P9-CZV-092

JACQUES MARITAIN

JACQUES MARITAIN

Homage in Words and Pictures

John Howard Griffin
and Yves R. Simon

Foreword by Anthony Simon

MAGI BOOKS, INC.

33 BUCKINGHAM DRIVE——ALBANY, NEW YORK 12208

ISBN 0-87343-046-8 ————— Library of Congress Card Number 73-85056

Some Books by John Howard Griffin: *Nuni*
Black Like Me
A Hidden Wholeness: The Visual World of Thomas Merton
Twelve Photographic Portraits
The Biography of Thomas Merton

Some Books by Yves R. Simon: *The Great Dialogue of Nature and Space*
Philosophy of Democratic Government
Freedom and Community
Freedom of Choice
Work, Society and Culture

Designed and executed by Rhoda Curley Palmieri

FOREWORD

My earliest recollections of Jacques Maritain originate about 1942. It was Christmas time and a present came for me in the mail, a small children's book, entitled *Saint Thomas Aquinas* by Raïssa Maritain. I was charmed by the illustrations in the book but puzzled by the inscription which read: "For Anthony Simon, for the beginning of his Thomistic library, from his dear friend Raïssa."

I quickly asked my parents: who is Raïssa? They of course explained that she was Madame Maritain, the wife of my father's greatest friend, Jacques Maritain. Thereafter all the Maritains, Jacques, Raïssa, and Véra were always a part of me. They were a real source of wonder and pride.

The original idea for the present book results from a long series of similar memories. All of my visits with the Maritains in New York, Princeton, Chicago, and South Bend built within me the legend of the Maritains and added to my sense within their presence of human greatness.

In 1938, the coming war was only a remote threat to us in the Midwest. Rereading my father's papers of that period, years later, I was struck by the confidence of his predictions on international affairs and how little such voices were heard then or much earlier. In letters to his great friend Edmond Michelet* (references will be found with asterisk in Note 6 to my father's essay), parts of which have recently been published, he wrote, twenty months before the June 1940 breakthrough:

Events now could go very fast. I do not know if France is still defendable after the destruction of the Czechoslovakian bastion. Now I do see coming the time when we shall have to surrender ourselves just as we have surrendered others . . . Do try something, members of Les Nouvelles Équipes Françaises, and know that if you fail, you will be going to concentration camps.

As Michelet recalls, "These reproving words from my friend were written four years before any Gestapo agent came to arrest me at the very house where I had received Yves Simon and his family . . ."

Again, in another letter to Michelet my father wrote on the twelfth of June 1940: "The Nazis will not win this war. It will be won by the United States of America; but God knows at what price . . ."

My early interests centered around art and history. I used to send rather primitive paintings to my godmother, Véra Oumançoff, Raïssa's sister, who always responded with unique encouragement. She wrote on the 10th of December 1942, in response to some painting I had sent, that she was overjoyed in my talent for art. She added that I should tell my father that the three Maritains were deeply moved by what he was writing about the life of the Maritains at Meudon in Canadian journals.*

The tragedy of the war years eventually brought many refugees to our home in South Bend; Paul Vignaux, Otto Von Simson, Waldemar Gurian, Charles Du Bos, Aloys Hermens and Karl Menger were but a few who had joined the Notre Dame scene. They all spoke warmly of Maritain. One had a sense that he had a unique mission, quite apart from the war, that was to be accomplished, in spite of the fact that politics preoccupied everyone during those precarious years. That mission was temporarily interrupted by the war, and obscured by the isolationist controversy that raged all around us.

I remember Henry Rago, the poet, on the eve of his departure for the European theater of the war saying, "It really doesn't matter where you meet the Maritains, in Paris, New York, Princeton, Chicago or South Bend, the same love of truth and culture exists wherever they are, that was so well known at Meudon."

During those early years of the war Maritain and my father laid aside theoretical philosophy, and poured their combined energy into helping refugees to escape and in writing political books and pamphlets to support the cause of the allies.

My father's war books, especially *The Road To Vichy* and *The March To Liberation*, prompted Maurice Schumann to call him "The Philosopher of the Fighting French." He was more pleased with that title than with an earlier label, "The Philosopher's Philosopher." A letter to my father in 1942 from General de Gaulle in London read:

I have received your letter of July 10 together with your book, *La Marche à la Délivrance*. I greatly appreciate your sending this writing and your dedication of the work to me. I am well aware of the activities in our favor which you are deploying for us from your present position.
There are many ways to serve France, yours is among the most effective . . .

Although Maritain and my father had been denied physical combat they had indeed become combatants. The price he had foreseen was being paid. Letters from Europe to Maritain and to my parents almost always brought news of the tragic plight of their friends who failed to elude the crushing hands of the Nazi regime. Michelet was captured and sent to Dachau along with the Bishop of Auvergne. It was hard for us as children in America to understand such continuous sadness for our parents and their friends.

Then it was over and a new sense of life was revived for both men. That goal of which I spoke, their unique mission, was to receive renewed attention with a concentrated vigor. New projects and books on philosophical topics were quickly in outline, while long-range plans were being formulated.

I remember a trip with my father to New York occasioned by Maritain's departure for Rome as French Ambassador to the Vatican. I was overwhelmed by my first encounter with that massive city, but utterly reassured by the affection and encouragement given so freely to me by the Maritains during our visit. We went out one evening — Maritain, my father and I — for dinner; they spoke for hours of mutual friends, many of whom were returning to postwar Europe. As I listened, I sensed my father's loneliness knowing Maritain also would soon leave.

The noted English actor Robert Speaight's great appreciation of Maritain results, I think, from what he sees as his mystical aestheticism, quite apart from any philosophical orientation. As my father indicates, Maritain was most often surrounded by poets and artists rather than by teachers and professors.

I spoke of this with Speaight during a recent visit in South Bend. He said that of course Maritain's penchant for beauty and art were well known to him long before he met Maritain at the home of John U. Nef in Chicago in 1940. The paradox for me was that Speaight felt my father was his most intimate friend at Notre Dame just before the fall of France. His temperament was quite the opposite of my father's, yet they spent evening after evening together, at our home, listening to the agonizing news broadcasts of events overseas. It seemed to console them both not to have to hear of the collapse of France alone.

My father's preoccupation with the war tended to be philosophical, historical and polemic. He had a keen and fascinating memory about the causes behind the collapse of France. I am sure that the outcome of international events during those years was made especially painful for my father because he so long foresaw, with an ominous precision, the path that they would take.

His memory was equally acute for recollections of a more personal nature. Memory was a subject which fascinated him. It seems impossible but he was convinced that he could give fine details of a great fire at his father's factory in Cherbourg, France, in 1905. He was at that time only two years old. I suggested to him that it was recall based upon hearing the same story as a child over and over. He was never convinced. Such a gift, in the end, was a great reward; he had only to think of his friends to really be with them. Among all of his cherished friendships, Maritain was central.

I remember his telling me that when he was a young student in Paris, he thought his burning desire to write meant his career would be literary. He did in fact write a few plays and poems but, one day, decided they were just awful. He quickly turned to philosophy after attending Maritain's classes at the Institut Catholique.

He loved to relate stories to me about his youth, during long lecture tours. I used to tag along on these trips, and heard wonderful stories about his friends and the famous personalities he had known. In retrospect, those early years and friendships with people of varied disciplines must have been just the perfect preparation for the development of his unique style of writing, which is so well known for its clarity and precision. The similarities between Maritain and my father, then, do really exist; both retained always a readiness to capture truth in any form. It was just that receptivity which captivated so many people no matter what their orientation and resulted in deep friendships which, on the surface, were difficult to explain.

After the war I developed a close friendship with Gerald B. Phelan, the founder of the Medieval Institute at the University of Toronto. Phelan was Maritain's first New World friend and responsible for his first lectures here. It was a joy for me in later years to have him give me informal tutorials on a few of Maritain's books. Phelan's diverse knowledge was overwhelming; he knew art, music and history as well as philosophy. He was a Renaissance man, totally human. His little book, *Jacques Maritain*, was the first on Maritain to be published in English.

After some flirtation with art, I turned my interests towards history. I was somewhat apprehensive to tell Maritain that I was giving up art and would now study history. My father urged me to spend an afternoon with Maritain at Notre Dame. He was asleep when I arrived, and tired, but after an hour's talk he understood perfectly my change of direction. I was relieved and greatly encouraged. This encouragement he continued to give all through my college years.

Just before one of Maritain's lectures the next day, he was told that he could speak as long as he liked. He turned to me in the corridor and asked, "Tony, help me: I don't understand." Somehow I managed to say quickly, in French, "Mr. Maritain, they want you to speak as long as you like. You can stop anytime." I was terribly proud to be of such small assistance. Later I drove him to our home for what was to be a long evening. Along the way he spoke delightfully of Véra and the impressions she had of me.

After hours of conversation at dinner I sensed and shared the joy it gave my parents to be with him. As we finished, my father asked, "Mr. Maritain you would be more comfortable in the study for coffee." Maritain turned to me and whispered, "Tony, look how he calls me after thirty years!" I shall never forget the warmth of that reaction with its slight resentment that any formality could exist between them. I excused myself and dashed to the corner drugstore to buy the finest cigars to offer him. It is the warmth of such friendships coupled with flashing intensity that are here captured by John Griffin's photographs and journal notes. I could always predict Maritain's reactions even when he was surrounded by skeptical scholars bent on asking mischievous questions. Those responses disarmed all of them, not so much by the weight of their cleverness but rather by their contagious warmth.

The essay on Maritain presented in this book was my father's last public lecture. It was for me a moving and unforgettable evening, one last tribute to his former teacher, friend, and brother-in-arms. Leo R. Ward* was there and shared our feelings on this unique occasion. He wrote later

Yves Simon . . . was one of the distinguished philosophers of the twentieth century. He was also an extraordinary teacher . . . Many students will say they never had a teacher to match him. He was sick for two years, but his devotion to teaching and study went right on. . . . Yves Simon felt that he was fortunate in meeting Jacques Maritain, a twentieth century philosopher whom he could take as his master. Even so, the discipline required has to be self-discipline: a man has to train himself. That is what Yves Simon did. . . . His last lecture was his most famous and most memorable. He was at that time a very sick man, but he had promised the lecture, and he lavished himself both on the preparation and the giving of it. It was touching and unforgettable. He could not walk or stand, and had to be carried onto the platform and propped up in pillows. He was suffering terribly. But the lecture did not suffer, and his hearers did not suffer. For two hours he lectured and answered questions with charm and with tremendous vigor, and every member of the audience, most of whom had never seen him before, waited and listened to every word.

I hope that this book, with the clarity of my father's perception of Maritain as a philosopher and the exquisite beauty of John Howard Griffin's photographs, will help all those who have known or will come to know Maritain, to relive the pleasure and promise that I have tried so briefly to express in this preface.

Future generations may well appreciate the complete charity, the greatness and the genius of this philosopher. Gilson has said that we have not yet begun to feel what Maritain has done for us. I have felt it for a long time. I cannot think of a better way of saying it than to borrow my father's words from an address he once gave for the presentation to Maritain of one of his many awards. Those words ended with the following:

I suggest a careful reading of his books. . . . Here you find a love of truth so intense and so pure as to make it plain that these works were written by a philosopher always ready to suspend his philosophic pursuit in order to help a fellow in need of a job, an outlaw in need of refuge, a soul in need of God.*

I should like to end with a note that I received from my godmother, Véra Oumançoff, in a copy of *Creative Intuition in Art and Poetry:*

For my dear godson, Anthony, who loves art and poetry.

Affectionately—

Véra

This book is but an attempt to touch lightly upon the surface of that art and that beauty which has surrounded the lives of the Maritains. John Howard Griffin and I would like to dedicate this book to my godmother, Véra Oumançoff, with all the warmth in which we cherish her memory.

Anthony O. Simon

South Bend, Indiana
1973

JACQUES MARITAIN: HOMAGE IN WORDS

Yves R. Simon

JACQUES MARITAIN

ONE of my duties as a member of the Committee on Social Thought of the University of Chicago is to help advanced students in the reading of philosophical classics. When the program of a student has included *Art and Scholasticism* or *A Preface to Metaphysics*, I have sometimes felt that I was able to clear up difficulties which might have been insuperable had I not had the privilege of personal acquaintance with Maritain and with the historical circumstances of his development.

These remarks suffice to give an idea of the subjects that I shall try to cover. The period is roughly that of the precarious peace between the two World Wars. I first heard of Maritain about 1920, when I became a university student. After we came to this country, I in 1938 and he in 1939, we no longer met frequently as we used to do in Paris.

To perceive what the historical context means in the development of Maritain, let us compare his career with that of Bergson. Bergsonian philosophy can be well understood without much information about the person of the philosopher and the circumstances under which his research took place. In fact, few people know much about Bergson's life and his relation to the history of his time. The exposition of his philosophy is very orderly; you would think that the day he planned out his doctoral dissertation he already knew what he would be writing at the age of seventy. This is a unique feat in the history of philosophy. We may be interested in knowing what kind of life was his: for a number of years he taught in secondary schools, then at the Ecole Normale Supérieure, then at the Collège de France. He retired in 1918. With some information about philosophic programs in the secondary schools of the French Republic, about the functions and customs of the Ecole Normale Supérieure, about the Collège de France and about philosophic trends in the late nineteenth century, we have almost all that the history of the times can contribute to the understanding of Bergson. The case of Maritain sharply contrasts with that of his teacher. As one goes ahead with the reading of Maritain's works, he constantly feels the need for more information about the occurrences with which the composition of his books and papers has been connected.

I would like to start with a paradox and say that Maritain was the first non-scholastic among the disciples of St. Thomas. Not long ago it was quite customary to speak of scholasticism as if there existed such a thing as a scholastic philosophy provided with doctrinal unity. In fact, there are at least half a dozen philosophic systems which have an equal right to be termed "scholastic," although they clash violently on a number of fundamental issues. Let us ask of what subjects the word "scholastic" can be predicated relevantly. Certainly not of a doctrine, but of a set of problems—what is called in German *eine Problematik*—of a method, of a language, of a cultural form, and, finally, of the period in which this *Problematik*, this method, this language and this cultural form were prevalent. It is particularly to scholasticism as a form of culture that Maritain referred when he wrote that the philosophy of St. Thomas is called scholastic from the name of its worst ordeal. A scholastic philosophy is a philosophy of professors, and Maritain holds that the professor is precisely the worst enemy of St. Thomas' philosophy. A scholastic culture is centered on what takes place between teachers and students, with little or no concern for what goes on in public affairs, in art and literature, and in spiritual life. It is this meaning of Scholasticism that we bear in mind when we set in contrast the Scholastics and the Humanists of the sixteenth century. These Scholastics were not always bad at expounding the rational, scientific and philosophic psychology of animals and man. But when there was a question of understanding man in the contingencies of history, in the indefinitely many accidents of his concrete existence, when there was a question of understanding what we now would call the existential man, they were rather poor, and the Humanists were much better. Interest in Scholastic philosophies was revived toward the end of the nineteenth century and the old conflict could be observed again. In fact, it had never died out. I know of liberal arts colleges where there is a tendency to center training about philosophy. Because of my professional interest, I might be expected to be enthusiastic about such programs. I am not. I rather think that on the college level it is man considered in the contingencies of his concrete existence who should be the main subject of liberal studies. Although there have been considerable changes in the attitudes and ideas of Maritain, one feature is present in all periods of his life: he has always been in warm contact with the existential man, and his excellence in the rational analysis of the soul has never interfered with his intuitive relation to men such as they are here and now, such as they have been shaped by history, by grace and by suffering, and such as they behave with regard to their eternal destiny.

These remarks lead us to consider Maritain's personal background. His family belonged to the most educated part of the bourgeoisie, and had connections with liberal Protestantism. He was born (1882) and raised in Paris. A city child, he may have retained some of the parochialism which is so common among Parisians. Léon Bloy was instrumental in the conversion of Maritain and his wife to the Catholic Church (1906).

The personality and the work of Bloy remain obscure subjects on which there is little literature of any value. Léon Bloy was in some respects a great writer; he was a man who suffered immensely and expressed human suffering with extraordinary intensity. His Catholic faith was deep, burning and uncompromising, with a definitely mystical direction. Here, we are touching upon a point which matters decisively for the understanding of Maritain and of the movements in which he was active. At some time in the history of the Church (I shall not dare to venture a date, but I suppose it was no later than the end of the seventeenth century) the feeling spread that religion was principally designed to procure the perfection of morality. This pragmatic interpretation was extremely common toward the end of the nineteenth century. It was frequent even among sincere believers. Where did it come from? To a large extent from a more or less explicit conviction that there was a conflict between religion and science and that, accordingly, religion should be defended in terms of helpfulness and fruitfulness, rather than in terms of truth. The thing that science cannot do is to take care of human sorrows and weaknesses, whereas religion brings strength and consolation.

I am aware of the weak points of Léon Bloy. His really good books are few. As a stylist he is very irregular. Some of his eccentricities are shocking. In his writings, personal names of contemporaries or transparent pseudonyms designate symbolic characters who happen to be charged with the most shameful actions. How does the reader know that such and such a name or pseudonym designates a symbol rather than a real man? But Léon Bloy was animated by the most burning conviction as he fought moralistic and pragmatic interpretations of religion. Few men contributed so effectively to the shaping of an era of pure faith. Under the influence of such a man as Bloy, the faithful understood better that the center of Christian life is the beatific vision of the Divine Persons and that, in this world, there is nothing greater than the contemplation of supernatural truth in the charity of Christ. At this point it is relevant to note that the great epistemological work of Maritain, *The Degrees of Knowledge*, which includes long chapters on the natural sciences, ends with studies on mystical experience. This association — infrequent in the history of epistemology — expresses a disposition which has been that of Maritain ever since his early progress in philosophy and in faith. He knows St. John of the Cross as well as St. Thomas Aquinas.

From the beginning Maritain had the soul of a contemplative and that of an artist. I have some notion of the people whose company he liked, for, over a long period, it was my privilege to visit his home on Sunday afternoons. The living room was generally crowded, less by teachers or students than by writers, poets, painters, musicians, persons interested in mysticism, missionaries and friends of the missions. Most of the artists were of the vanguard description. Concerning Maritain's philosophical education, the important fact is that he studied under Bergson. The level of philosophical work in French universities was then at an all-time low. The predominance of neo-positivism and neo-criticism did not allow much philosophical thought to survive. Commenting on Bergson's doctoral dissertation, which is known in English as *Time and Free Will* but whose original title is *Essay on the Immediate Data of Consciousness* (1889), Georges Sorel wrote that the work of Bergson stood like a green and vigorous oak tree over the wasteland of contemporary philosophy. In Bergson's classroom a brilliantly gifted young man felt that philosophy was still capable of great accomplishments.

We noticed that one of the things of which "scholastic" can be relevantly predicated is a certain language. To be sure, some scholastic writers must be praised for having worked out a vocabulary equal to that of the exact sciences in precision and definiteness. But philosophic disciplines are things so human that they can hardly do without beauty of expression. The awakening of philosophic thought, as well as its communication, often requires the help of poetry. Scholastic writings are notorious for lacking the very qualities of style that philosophy needs if it is to be really alive and to achieve steady progress. This state of affairs was particularly shocking in France, where modern philosophy was founded by great writers. The school of St. Thomas badly needed a man capable of writing with art. Scholastic style is bad enough in Latin, but, when it is put in the vernacular, it is generally atrocious.

Maritain soon displayed qualities of intuitive, poetic and thought-provoking expression. However, the circumstances of his calling often made it impossible for him to get the best out of his talents as a writer. For one reason or another, most of his papers and books had to be completed within deadlines. Like Bergson, he could have won much glory in the art of writing. No doubt it has been in full awareness that he has consented to publish, for the service of men, many pages which fall short of the perfection of literary form he could have given them if he had been less interested in the urgent expression of truth. It is not always good to let souls wait until rough material has been polished, until long sentences have been nicely divided and until remarks placed in parentheses or brackets have been harmoniously integrated. In spite of difficult circumstances, there are pages of great beauty in all the works of Maritain. The long preface to the second edition of his book on Bergson demonstrates best his power as an artist. These eighty-six pages are a thing of beauty, where one could hardly find any defect.

Maritain has been and remains a nonspecialized philosopher. He has done important work in all parts of philosophy. He is the author of a treatise of formal logic, which was supposed to be followed by a volume of material logic that circumstances never allowed him to write. In several parts of his work there are essays belonging to the philosophy of inanimate nature, to the philosophy of life, to psychology; and everybody knows how voluminous is his contribution in metaphysics, ethics, and politics. True, of the many volumes which make up his works, only a few have the kind of unity that such a well-organized mind was capable of achieving. Not by choice, most of Maritain's books are made up of lectures and essays. He was often needed as a speaker and, rightly or wrongly, he always believed that he had no gift for extemporaneous speech. Almost all his lectures were written from the first to the last word. I am even tempted to say that most of the time what he did for his audiences was not to deliver a lecture but rather to read a booklet. A few weeks later the booklet, carefully revised and generally expanded, would be published as a journal article, and eventually, after considerable work toward completeness and greater accuracy, a few articles would be published in book form. Some of Maritain's best books would seem to be poorly constructed if we did not know that the real unit is not the book itself but each of the essays that have become its chapters. The great book entitled *The Degrees of Knowledge* (1932) is by no means a treatise on the degrees of knowledge. It is a collection of papers written as lectures about philosophy and experimental science, about the meaning of critical realism, about the greatness and the poverty of metaphysics, and about philosophy and mystical experience. All these papers have been revised with extreme care and the reader does not, at any time, feel that his expectation is frustrated by lack of order. *The Degrees of Knowledge* would be something completely different if it had been conceived as a systematic and complete treatise. I am not sure that it would have been better. The method actually followed by Maritain may have given him the best chance to fulfill his calling, which was not so much to treat questions without discontinuity as to awaken philosophical understanding in a great variety of domains and to demonstrate what the philosophy of St. Thomas is able to do for us in the difficulties, the possibilities and the yearnings of our time. Let it be remarked, however, that when Maritain wanted to write, not one essay after another, but a genuine book, planned as a book from the first day, he succeeded beautifully. The first edition of *Art and Scholasticism* is a masterwork of organization. In later editions, organization is somewhat weakened by the addition of more papers on art, on poetry and on beauty. But these papers we like to have under the same cover as *Art and Scholasticism*. True, the disadvantages of short compositions disappear, for the most part, when they are put together according to subjects. If we want to know about the theory of the sciences, we are certainly going to read *The Degrees of Knowledge*. The better informed will also read *Science and Wisdom*. But who would suspect that there is a paper on this subject in a book entitled *Scholasticism and Politics*? It is our hope that the Jacques Maritain Center at Notre Dame will accomplish the work of reorganization which matters so much for the influence of Maritain in the future. The task is worthy: let us not forget that since 1644—the date of John of St. Thomas' death—there has been only one man of genius among the followers of St. Thomas.

We now propose to describe the subjects where Maritain's gifts of intuitive familiarity are at their best. This critic of Bergson, this philosopher who spent so much of his life explaining and vindicating conceptual knowledge and who never missed a chance to use those "scholastic distinctions" that ignoramuses mistake for vain subtleties, gives evidence of a mind in which philosophic discovery and progress are constantly enhanced by the intuitions of the contemplative, the artist, the believer, and the man of charity.

First comes metaphysics, which abounds in all of Maritain's writings. For its central position, its thought-provoking power, its liveliness and constant association of science and poetry, I recommend *A Preface to Metaphysics* (original title: *Seven Lectures on Being and the First Principles of Theoretical Reason*, 1934). Written in "spoken" language, these seven lectures were taken in shorthand and later somewhat polished, but the style of oral exposition was intentionally retained.

Maritain was still very young when he wrote *Art and Scholasticism. The Responsibility of the Artist* on the other hand was published in 1960. I expect him to write papers on art and beauty until his last day. Thus, many are still to come if our prayers are listened to. Let our attention now be directed to a paradox of great significance. That an artist should be interested in scholasticism, should find a philosophy of art in St. Thomas, Cajetan, and John of St. Thomas, and should use the principles of this philosophy to understand and explain what is going on in the vanguard of painting, music and poetry in the twentieth century, will remain one of the best surprises that ever confronted historians of philosophy. What "scholasticism" meant when Maritain was a young man has become hard to realize, precisely because of the work he has been doing, for half a century, especially in the domain of the philosophy of art. "Scholasticism" was never in vital communication with the living energies of temporal communities. Even at its best it was an academic and ecclesiastical affair. (The name of Descartes does not appear in John of St. Thomas' *Courses* of philosophy and theology any more than the name of John of St. Thomas appears in the works of Descartes.) At the beginning of the present century, "Scholasticism" suffered from having been deprived of genius for two and a half centuries. The monks and seminary professors who delivered and published courses of "scholastic" philosophy were not all inept, and we should not find it below our dignity to learn from such teachers as Zigliara and San Severino. Men like these two really believe what they teach, and their erudition is useful. Their metaphysical thought is by no means lifeless, but the thing that they cannot achieve is to impart a new life to metaphysics. In the great universities of the world it was generally taken for granted that there existed no such thing as a science of metaphysics; no professor of the Sorbonne or of the University of Berlin had ever heard such names as

San Severino or Zigliara. In fact, what was going on in philosophy departments at the turn of the century was generally not very important. The genius of Western nations was producing masterworks in history, the sciences, technology and the fine arts, but there was no communication between these domains of intellectual vitality and the sound work that a few seminary teachers offered to the world in a very particular language. It has been said that a word is "a little poem born of the people's spontaneity." Such poems are absent from the best as well as from the worst products of "scholastic" philosophy in the nineteenth century. After having read the first essays of Maritain on Bergson, Léon Bloy wrote in his diary that philosophy had quite a new appearance when it was treated by his godson. "[I have] read in the *Revue Thomiste* a paper of my godson Jacques Maritain, 'The Two Bergsonisms.' That I have little use for philosophy is well known: In my opinion it is the most boring way of wasting the precious time of our lives and its Hyrcanian dialect discourages me. But with Jacques Maritain things are strikingly different . . . It never occurred to me that the shabby jacket of a philosopher could clothe such a strong arm. The arm is that of an athlete and the voice expresses a powerful lamentation. I felt at the same time something like a wave of sorrowful poetry, a mighty wave coming from very far."

Together with metaphysics and the philosophic reflection on art, mystical life is one of the areas where Maritain is most at home and exercises, as it were effortlessly, his intuitive gifts. The importance of the studies on mysticism in *The Degrees of Knowledge* cannot be exaggerated. It is good that there should be a book in which the ways proper to mystical experience, as well as those proper to the positive sciences, are compared with those of philosophy and theology. It is good, in particular, that a philosopher should have taken the trouble of explaining to us how the sentences of a theologian and those of a mystical writer may express agreement at a very deep level although they sound contradictory. Such explanation could be given only by a philosopher familiar with the great epistemological notions of formal abstraction, degree of abstraction, standpoint, formal and material object, formal object *quod* and formal object *quo*. As already noted, Maritain knows St. John of the Cross as well as he knows St. Thomas. These two geniuses use considerably different methods of thought and expression. St. Thomas says that judgment about things divine may proceed by way of cognition—the result is scientific theology, the sacred doctrine—or by way of inclination—the result is mystical experience (*Sum. Theol.*, I. 1, 6.ad 3.). Maritain is familiar with both of these ways. It is for very good reasons that the full title of *The Degrees of Knowledge* is *Distinguish to Unite or The Degrees of Knowledge.*

I have mentioned three areas marked by the excellence of intuitive familiarity. In other domains, Maritain did an immense amount of work whose quality is often equal to that of the work done in these three distinguished areas. The difference concerns less the work done by the writer than the work to be done by the reader. Granted that the case of a dull or lazy reader is hopeless anyway, it should be said that in such a domain as art, understanding is powerfully aided by the intuitive warmth of the text. When Maritain writes about mathematics, physics, and politics, what he says may be deeply true and valuable in many respects, but the reader is not helped by the warmth of intuitive familiarity as he would be if the subject were art or mysticism.

The lecture on philosophy and experimental science which became one of the most important chapters of *The Degrees of Knowledge* was given about 1925. Here, while ceaselessly concerned with uniting the efforts of the mind toward truth, Maritain shows by what vital operations the study of the physical world splits into two ways of thought: one is properly described as philosophic, and the other is commonly called scientific. I am happy to say that an important reason why I followed the teaching of Maritain more than that of any other contemporary philosopher is precisely his treatment of the relation between science and philosophy.[1] In recent years, controversies on those subjects have been violent, and Maritain's positions were attacked with a somewhat paradoxical zeal. Why is it that while diversity has been asserted by the constant direction of scholarly labor over generations and centuries, an aspiration in plain conflict with the stream of history continues to appeal successfully to many minds? When this question is clearly stated, it is easy to see that Maritain's position and that of his most intelligent opponents do not diverge so sharply as some believe. The truth is that the ideas expressed in *The Degrees of Knowledge* on the science and the philosophy of nature were only the beginning of a doctrine which urgently called for further elaboration, perhaps by its originator and certainly by his students. But after the publication of *The Degrees of Knowledge*, Maritain's enormous capacity for work was almost entirely dedicated to other subjects. As for his students, they were few, and they did not do the job.

The writings on politics may be, at the present time, the most celebrated and widely-discussed part of Maritain's work. It is important to remember that he came quite late to political and related subjects. Prior to 1926, his writings contain scattered allusions to political ideas which were in the air. Almost simultaneously we notice these new and consequential occurrences: for one thing, Maritain's creative interest comes to include the philosophy of societies; for another, from now on, a great part of his philosophic work will be concerned with the public events of the day. To ascertain the meaning of Maritain's writings in politics, to understand his dispositions as an observer of public events and the style of his expositions, it is indispensable to keep in mind that his career as a social and political thinker began when he was nearing forty-five. It is still more important to remember that the events which occasioned the new directions of his work were grave and, in more than one respect, heartbreaking. In 1926, the movement called *L'Action française* went into a crisis and soon was condemned by the Church. It is difficult to recount this strange story in its entirety (save in the roughest outline), much less to explain it. Some aspects of the case remain obscure and are likely never to be clarified quite satisfactorily.[2]

By the time I went to Paris as a university student (1920), *Action française* was constantly gaining influence among intellectuals. It was a school of thought and a league rather than a party. Founded in the last years of the nineteenth century, its program was the restoration of traditional monarchy. But the word *program* is not strong enough, for the faith of the *Action française* people, and their readiness to take the words of their leaders were such that the restoration of monarchy in France (after a few years of daily excitement) had become the all-embracing solution to the problem of evil.

The daily paper, entitled *L'Action française,* was directed and, to a large extent, composed by two writers of great distinction, Léon Daudet and Charles Maurras. The son of a famous novelist, Daudet was himself the author of a few novels, but he was far better at writing memoirs and polemics. Maurras was the doctrinal leader of the school. It is hard to say what kind of thinker and what kind of man he was. In spite of highly dignified manners which resembled those of a philosopher, his interests were not philosophical in any technical sense. Rather, he was a classicist, an artist whose ideals were derived from Greek and Latin patterns. He could also be a powerful journalist. The deepest feature of his intellectual personality was perhaps the ideal of a state conceived as a work of art and governed by rules akin to those of the fine arts. The literary level of the whole enterprise was so excellent that if you had any feeling for French literature, you could have a pleasant breakfast every morning by reading the daily editorials of *Action française,* even though you might detest its ideas.

The movement was widely different from the various royalist groups which, despite the steady progress of republican ideas in nearly all parts of the nation, had never died out. It did not have the conservative, traditionalistic, upperclass, and aristocratic externals without which other royalist groups would have been inconceivable. With regard to religion, the make-up and the positions of *Action française* were somewhat paradoxical. It was the most outspoken adversary of republican anticlericalism and of the "secular laws" to which the French Republic was so firmly devoted. Yet Charles Maurras was a complete agnostic. As a result of his cult of classical antiquity, he was known to have written a few pages of definitely pagan and anti-Christian inspiration. There were practicing Catholics among the leaders of the movement. Léon Daudet was one of them. Others were reputed to have no religion and even to be hostile to Christianity. In the years to which we are referring, the influence of *Action française* in the Catholic world was great. Most of the theologians who were friends of Maritain were also, almost as a matter of course, friends of *Action française* and indeed there was a time when a Thomist opposed to this movement looked eccentric, undependable, and rather ridiculous. Few cared to assume such an appearance.

In the summer of 1926, the Archbishop of Bordeaux published a letter exhorting the youth to keep away from *Action française,* whose influence was described, in very severe terms, as a danger to the essence of the Christian spirit. This document was shortly followed by a letter of the Pope to the Archbishop. While emphasizing the freedom of Catholics with regard to forms of government, Pope Pius XI approved the effort of the Archbishop of Bordeaux to check the influence of *Action française,* especially among the youth. An extremely bitter and violent crisis developed rapidly. On September 19, 1926, Maritain published his first political writing, a pamphlet entitled *An Opinion on Charles Maurras and the Duty of the Catholics.* At that time, what was meant to be obligatory in the Pope's directions was not entirely clear. But following the outright revolt of *Action française,* the daily paper as well as several books of Maurras were soon placed on the Index of Forbidden Books (December 29, 1926). The Catholics of *Action française* responded, roughly, in three ways. Some submitted reluctantly and kept their submission at a minimum. Others did not submit at all and for thirteen years remained in a state of rebellion. Many however submitted generously. To these the understanding of the case, so difficult at the beginning, came gradually. Out of an act of painful obedience, the loftiest kind of freedom was born for a number of souls.

Maritain never had had any formal connection with the now-condemned organization. But *Action française* had often praised him as a philosopher and had, indeed, contributed to the success of his early works. In 1922, the book *Antimoderne* was reviewed by Léon Daudet in his two-column, first-page editorial. As far as I remember, the job was quite well done and certainly helped to make Maritain known to a relatively large public. It is perhaps mostly because of the way *Action française* had recommended him that when the crisis came, Maritain felt it a duty to help puzzled minds and souls in peril. Prior to the condemnation of the movement, he had published the already-mentioned pamphlet on the duty of Catholics in which a sharp criticism of Maurras did not prevent him from voicing the hope that conditions of peace could still be provided. After the condemnation came *The Things That Are Not Caesar's* (original title: *Primacy of the Spiritual*). This book contained both theological studies on the relations of Church and State, and a timely, practical, apostolic, and fraternal message to beloved souls in the darkness of their ordeal. It soon became obvious to many that the effect of "Primacy" was profound and would be lasting. Today we realize that a new era had been opened, the characteristics of which were an ardent quest for theological enlightenment, an uncompromising sense of the intrinsic excellence and the irreducible worth of the temporal common good, and, finally, a burning zeal for the duty of helping, with all the resources of charity, humility, and knowledge, souls who could not wait, since they were engaged in a conflict involving eternity. In the years to come, situations characterized by darkness, by devotion to the temporal city, by an overwhelming sense of the primacy of things eternal, and by a loving understanding of the uniqueness of a personal calling in the midst of common anguish, were to occur again and again. The precedent set by *Primacy of the Spiritual* was to be followed by many more words ardently directed toward the understanding of what was going on in an immensely suffering world. Despite some appearances, and the very intense activity of theological wisdom and apostolic charity, the writings of Maritain would remain those of a philosopher whose effort always is, in some way or other, centered on problems natural, human, and temporal. Even in his strongest assertions concerning the primacy of the spiritual, Maritain would be faithful to the philosopher's calling with all that it implies regarding the natural character of the wisdom to be worked out in the midst of ordeals which involve our supernatural destiny.

The crisis of *Action française* ended only in 1939, with a formula of submission and repentance. Many things had happened in the meantime. I feel that I am no longer young when I see all around me boys and girls to whom the Spanish Civil War does not mean so much. It is already an old story. How many Spaniards died in this war? One million is a reasonable estimate, and a rather conservative one. The thing that I cannot say is what fraction of that million died on the battlefield. Beyond doubt, the ratio of those killed outside of all military action was very high. Whenever someone says that a huge amount of crime was committed only on the other side, he either lies or does not know all the facts. Besides the slaughter, the Spanish Civil War brought about, and not in Spain alone, an extraordinary indulgence in hatred and in the most debased feelings the human soul ever conceived. The French were close to the Spanish War in more than one respect. Lies about every subject that pertained to the ordeal of Spain were really atrocious. Spanish refugees who were pouring into France comprised all sorts of characters, from the most noble to the most undependable. We all felt that we had an urgent duty to do something about the misfortune of our neighbors and its international consequences. Maritain stood for mediation between the parties at war. So did I.

We met in committees with a faint hope that the crushing victory of one side and the slaughter of the other might be avoided. Anyway, committees were needed to organize some sort of aid for refugees. Besides works of relief, this much at least could be attempted: to save a few souls from systematic falsehood. Once more Maritain was taken into the world of action by the demands of truth and of charity. The effect of such circumstances on political thinking is obvious. Political philosophers and theologians have a tendency to oversimplify things and to derive obnoxious satisfaction from the host of illusions that their lack of experience renders inevitable. As the Spanish Civil War was going on, Maritain could not even be tempted to write papers or books on the abstract behavior of political and social essences. The circumstances made it necessary for his quickly-maturing political thought to stay in the midst of particular facts. The interest that he was then developing was especially concerned with historical trends. (His most important writing in this connection is his long preface to the book of Alfredo Mendizabal, *The Martyrdom of Spain.* 1938.)[3]

Indeed, a social or political essence cannot afford to exist without being marked by the contingency of factual situations. If we study, for instance, the relation between the temporal and the spiritual powers, let it be understood, from the beginning, that whatever is essential and necessary in this relation is always accompanied by features which do not belong in essential, necessary and universal fashion to the relation between the spiritual and the temporal. When such issues are considered practically—and this is the proper way to consider them, for they are practical issues—the feature born of contingency may be of decisive significance. Accordingly, it is most unreasonable to assume that a problem such as, say, the relation of Church and State, admits of basically identical solutions in Spain and in Ireland, or in the Spain of the seventeenth century and in that of our time. Generally speaking, to assume that an analysis of essences can ever suffice to take care of an issue modified by contingency, in other words, to assume that moral science can deal with contingent matters without being supplemented by the virtue of prudence, is a silly illusion which should not have survived the criticism of Socrates by Aristotle. But prudence, as philosophers and theologians understand it, is a kind of wisdom so hard to get, to keep and to manage, that under a variety of names mankind is likely always to nurture the ideal of a science which would suffice to trace our way in this world of contingency.

These are elementary remarks, and yet no more is needed to make the philosopher feel very uncertain about his role in human communities. After it is clearly understood that no scientific method will answer a question relative, in any way whatsoever, to contingent data, it soon becomes easy to understand that the philosopher, far from being able to answer *philosophically* the questions which puzzle his fellow citizens, may well be at a disadvantage and have particular reasons to remain silent. In order to acquire any kind of social and political prudence, a great deal of human experience is necessary. But a philosopher is a man who has spent his youth in libraries, in classrooms, in laboratories, in museums, and other such places where opportunities for human experience are at a minimum. It seems that the question is decided by these simple remarks: far from owing to his knowledge distinguished abilities for making judgments about the affairs of the community, the philosopher would be almost inevitably bound, by the circumstances of his career, to be a poorly-trained citizen, who should feel diffident when he is tempted to take part in public affairs. Of course, this would not prevent him from joining committees and exercising charity when, as a result of a civil war, hungry women and children are looking for help in a country where it is still possible to find food and shelter.

But this is only one side of the story, as I was led to understand by an incident of my own career. My first political writing, if I omit a few articles in my student years, was a short study on the Ethiopian War, or more exactly on the attitudes of French political thinkers toward Mussolini's war in Ethiopia.[4] As this pamphlet was about to be published, I happened to describe it to an old friend whom I had known in groups formed for the study of international organizations. He was a man of sharp intelligence and fine education, a jurist by training, and a civil servant of high rank. Some prominent and noisy intellectuals had just given Mussolini the support of an enthusiastic manifesto. My friend listened attentively to my exposition. He interrupted me with this remark: "*You* are trained in the handling of abstract ideas." In another context this remark would have meant that a philosopher is restricted to abstractions and has no sense of political contingencies. But this is not what he had in mind. He plainly meant that to fulfill such a task as the defense of public conscience against corruption by politicians and intellectuals a few so-called abstract ideas, e.g., those of right, law, contract, community, authority, force, legal coercion, violence, autonomy, and civilization have got to be handled, and that in order that they be handled properly, philosophical training is necessary, or very helpful. To answer the question as to whether philosophers ever have a duty to take a stand with regard to temporal events such as a war, a revolution, a persecution, or the condemnation of an innocent person, we need only to understand the simple remark that my friend did me the honor of making on the occasion of my pamphlet. In order that the duties of prudence be fulfilled, it is sometimes necessary that the prudent man should have more than a commonsense ability to handle "abstract ideas." The need for such ability is still more obvious when there is a question of contributing as much truth as possible to the visions which animate a community, to its *ideology*—if this word can be freed from all unfavorable connotations.

Maritain was well trained in the handling of abstract ideas. Furthermore, he had a religious and mystical sense for the relation of time to eternity. He had all that prudence required, over and above the properly prudential qualities, in order that devotion to truth and justice should be worthily represented in a dialogue in which the most brutish appetites were both hidden and strengthened by the power of "abstract ideas" and of corrupt mysticism.

To accomplish the task we are trying to characterize, the understanding of historical trends is decisively important. An "historical trend" is the behavior of a social or political essence as modified by a situation which, in spite of its contingency, covers and governs a long period over large areas of human communities. When an historical trend is properly identified, it can be safely said that, as things go on, its characteristic features will be more and more unmistakably determined. And thus, within an order of things marked by contingency, we have to deal with a system which, as far as the purposes of action are concerned, assumes a character of necessity almost as definite as that of an essential type. It can be said, without any disorderly indulgence in metaphor, that the possible behaviors of a social or political essence are restricted to a small number of forms. Whoever has identified an historical trend has understood the law of the form which will predominate, again, over large areas and over long periods. Besides all that pertained to the immediate service of truth and charity against stubborn falsehood and hatred, the work of Maritain, in relation to the Spanish Civil War, consisted mostly in understanding what types of behavior had been assumed, in the lasting contingency of ages marked by such events as the Reformation, the Liberal Revolution, and Socialism, by such an issue as the relation between Church and State, and by such an ideal as that of the Christian State.

A student told me some time ago that he disliked in Maritain the constant association of the philosophic discourse with the apostolic concern. What my answer was I do not remember, but I think I know what it should have been. For one thing, I should have remarked that most readers and auditors are themselves so interested in the connections between philosophy and religion that they do not want philosophical problems to be treated in isolation, that is, apart from the religious issues to which they are related vitally, though not essentially, in the longing of men for the truths which matter most in terms of human destiny. The thing which cannot be tolerated under any circumstances is that orders be confused, and that philosophic issues be treated according to revealed principles without a plain statement that we are no longer in philosophy. But such a confusion—a frequent accident, indeed, in the history of Christian thought—is particularly repugnant to a Thomist. In the discussions which have been going on for over thirty years on the notion of "Christian philosophy," Maritain has never failed to recall, against any possible misunderstanding, that this expression designates a *state* of philosophy, not an essence. If it is designated an essence, it would be granted that philosophy receives premises from revelation, and of the great statements of St. Thomas concerning philosophy, theology, and their relationship, nothing would be left. When these positions are clearly formulated, the question remains as to whether it is desirable that philosophical issues be treated in a state of abstraction or in a concrete condition of association with the problems of our supernatural destiny. I would not hesitate to say that it is, to a large extent, a question of calling. I am strongly attracted by the method of isolation because it furnishes special guaranties of epistemological purity and logical rigor. To be sure, Maritain will never be tempted to use a revealed premise in a philosophical treatment. But there can be no doubt that his calling is that of the Christian philosopher who generally treats philosophical issues in the particular *state* that they assume by reason of their relation to Christian faith and theology.

Likewise, when we come to practical issues, it may be asked whether it is desirable that what is essential and scientific in them should be treated in the state of scientific isolation, or in association with problems of a prudential nature. Again, the answer is, to a large extent, determined by one's particular calling. In order that we should, at all times, be aware of what we are doing, in order that epistemological purity be preserved, it is certainly desirable that some men should write treatises of political philosophy or theology where the consideration of contingency and the decisions of prudence play as small a part as possible. But what the calling of Maritain was is not dubious. We have seen that all his writings on political and social subjects were composed under circumstances which, purely and simply, demanded an extensive exercise of historical intelligence and prudential judgment.

In this long exposition, little has been said about the moral personality of Maritain.[5] What would have been the use of expressing admiration for a man to whom I am well known to owe so much? By way of conclusion, I wish, however, to remark that there may well be a difference between the calling of a man and his choice. By "choice" I mean what he would have chosen if he had had his own way. I suspect that there have been many conflicts throughout Maritain's career between his choice and his calling. And I cannot think of a single case in which his calling was not preferred to his choice. Remote ages may find it relevant to remark that Maritain is the philosopher who, in case of conflict, never hesitated to fulfill his calling rather than to follow his choice.[6]

NOTES

This essay originally appeared in a slightly different form as "Jacques Maritain: The Growth of a Christian Philosopher," in *Jacques Maritain: The Man and His Achievement,* ed. Joseph W. Evans (New York: Sheed and Ward, 1936), pp. 3-24. It is used here with permission. The footnotes have been added by Anthony O. Simon.

1. See Simon's classic essay on "Maritain's Philosophy of the Sciences." It has appeared in the following: *The Thomist,* V (January, 1943),

85-102; Jacques Maritain, *The Philosophy of Nature* (New York: Philosophical Library, 1951), pp. 157-182; *The Philosophy of Physics*, ed. Vincent E. Smith, St. John's University Studies, No. 2 (New York: St. John's University Press, 1961), pp. 25-39.

2. The most important book on this subject is by Joseph Ungen Weber, *Action Française: Royalism and Reaction in Twentieth Century France* (California: Stanford University Press, 1962).

3. Alfred Mendizabal, *The Martyrdom of Spain* (New York: Charles Scribner's Sons, 1938).

4. Yves R. Simon, *La campagne d'Ethiopie et la pensée politique Française* (2nd ed.; Paris: Desclée de Brouwer, 1937). English translation in preparation.

5. The *Jacques Maritain Center* of the University of Notre Dame is the depository of the correspondence between Jacques Maritain and Yves R. Simon from 1920 to 1961. It is expected that they will be published. These letters contain lengthy discussions on various philosophical topics as well as a wealth of biographic material on both men.

6. For a bibliography of Maritain's works see Donald and Idella Gallagher, *The Achievement of Jacques and Raïssa Maritain* (New York: Doubleday and Company, 1962).

For a bibliography of Yves Simon's works see Anthony O. Simon, "Yves R. Simon: A Bibliography 1923-1970," in Yves R. Simon, *Work, Society and Culture*, ed. Vukan Kuic (New York: Fordham University Press, 1971), pp. 189-228.

Other works on Jacques Maritain by Yves R. Simon are: *"Pour le soixantième anniversaire de Jacques Maritain," *La Nouvelle Relève*, Montréal, Vol. II, No. 2 (décembre, 1942), 66-69. *"La philosophie dans la foi: Extrait des mémoires d'un philosophe Française," *La Nouvelle Relève*, Montréal, Vol. I, No. 5 (février, 1942), 257-265; and Vol. I, No. 6 (mars, 1942), 336-342. "On the Common Good," *The Review of Politics*, Vol. VI, No. 4 (October, 1944), 530-533. *"Jacques Maritain," *U.S. Catholic*, Vol. XXXIV, No. 1 (May, 1968), 43-44. "La philosophie bergsonienne—Étude critique," *Revue de Philosophie, N.S.*, tome II (juillet, 1931) 281-290.

For some tributes to Yves R. Simon see: James A. Corbett, "Yves Simon at Notre Dame," *Notre Dame Alumnus*, Vol. 49, No. 5 (October, 1971), 8-9. Donald A. Gallagher, "Yves R. Simon: Retrospect and Prospect," *Revue de l'Université d'Ottawa*, Vol. 41, No. 4 (octobre-décembre, 1971), 513-517. Francis L. Gammon, "The Philosophical Thought of Yves R. Simon: A Brief Survey," *Revue de l'Université d'Ottawa*, Vol. 42, No. 2 (avril-juin, 1972), 237-244. Olivier Lacombe, "Yves Simon," *Revue de l'Université d'Ottawa*, Vol. 42, No. 1 (janvier-mars, 1972), 5-7. Jacques Maritain, "Yves Simon," *Jubilee*, Vol. 9, No. 4 (August, 1961), 2-3. *Edmond Michelet, "Mon Ami Yves R. Simon," *Listening Magazine* (Dubuque, Iowa), Vol. 5, Nos. 2-3 (Autumn, 1970), 145-153; "Mon Ami Yves Simon," *Nova et Vetera*, Vol. XLIII, No. 3 (juillet-septembre, 1968), 208-213. J. Stanley Murphy, "Yves Simon and the Free World," *Revue de l'Université d'Ottawa*, Vol. 42, No. 2 (avril-juin, 1972), 245-251. John U. Nef, "Yves R. Simon and the University of Chicago," *The University of Chicago Magazine*, Vol. LXIV, No. 5 (May-June, 1972), 37. Rufus W. Rauch, Jr. "Yves Simon," *Notre Dame Alumnus*, Vol. 49, No. 6 (December, 1971), 50. Clare Riedl, "Yves Simon—Philosopher," *Revue de l'Université d'Ottawa*, Vol. 42, No. 2 (avril-juin, 1972), 232-236. Paule Simon, "The Papers of Yves R. Simon," *The New Scholasticism*, Vol. 38, No. 4 (October, 1963), 501-507. Pierre-Henri Simon, "Yves Simon," *Revue de l'Université d'Ottawa*, Vol. 42, No. 2 (avril-juin, 1972), 227-231. Anthony O. Simon and Patricia Fenelon, "Yves Simon Papers," *University of Notre Dame Library Newsletter*, Vol. 4, No. 2-3 (February, 1972), 3-6. Gerard Smith, "Yves R. Simon," *Renascence*, Vol. XXV, No. 3 (Spring, 1972), 72-76. Robert Speaight, "Yves R. Simon—Friend and Ally," *The Catholic World*, Vol. 211, No. 1266, (September, 1970), 268-269. Paul Vignaux, "Par delà l'experience du désespoir," *Revue Philosophique de Louvain*, 5th Series, tome 70, No. 6 (mai, 1972), 192-196. *Leo R. Ward, "Yves Simon—Philosopher," *Commonweal*, Vol. LXXIV, No. 14 (June 30, 1961), 351-352.

JACQUES MARITAIN: HOMAGE IN PICTURES

Diary and Photographs

by

John Howard Griffin

Princeton

October 26, 1962   ARRIVED LAST EVENING, or really early this morning after lectures in Illinois and finally found a room at the Nassau Inn, a nice place but very expensive. I have the day to rest and will see Jacques at ten tomorrow morning for a couple of hours. It seems impossible after all these years of intimate correspondence that this visit has worked out, and it would not have if Father Stan Murphy, C.S.B., had not insisted and even lent me the money to come here. We feel that it may well be our last chance to be together.

Princeton is beautiful as I had been told it would be. A cold, overcast day, some snow, trees flamboyantly colorful. Spent most of the day walking and looking. The prices of things frighten me, however. To economize, this evening I went to a delicatessen and bought salami (9 thick slices) and some excellent rolls for 34 cents and a quarter pound of butter for 19 cents. And I had a feast—three good sandwiches for less than it would cost to get a cheese sandwich in a restaurant. And enough left for tomorrow.

This evening I telephoned M. F. Ashley-Montagu and spent an hour with him and his wife in their home. Am to return to photograph him tomorrow after my visit with Jacques. He showed me some magnificent photos of himself with Einstein taken by Roth.

October 27   The taxi arrived to pick me up at 9:30 this morning. I asked for 26 Linden Lane and after we had driven several blocks through the beautiful streets of Princeton, the driver asked: "How is Dr. Maritain?" He explained that he had often picked up Jacques or Raïssa at that address, but had not seen Jacques now in some time. "He's a great old gentleman," he remarked. "I've always enjoyed driving him."

We arrived in front of the modest two-story house at 9:50, so I decided to remain outside until exactly ten before ringing the bell. I deposited my heavy camera bag with its Leicas and extra lenses against the pillar of the large front porch and walked in the clear autumn sunlight to the end of the tree-lined block and back.

At ten I rang the bell and it was answered almost immediately by a small, troubled-looking lady whom I took to be Jacques' housekeeper. She knew me, was expecting me, and began to lament that I would have to walk up the stairs with my bad legs — or no, perhaps Jacques could come down, though he was supposed to stay in bed until noon. She spoke in a rapid, elegant French, getting more and more agitated as I tried to reassure her that I would climb many flights of stairs with pleasure to see Jacques. She hurried upstairs and I heard her speak to Jacques in a loud voice. They used the "tu" form, so I knew she was not just a housekeeper.

I climbed to the top of the stairs and waited in the vestibule as she and Jacques made rapid arrangements for him to get up and come down the stairs. When she saw I was there already, she called back into his room that there was no need for him to get up now. She opened the door to a tiny room, well-lighted by windows at the foot of the bed. In that narrow, single bed, the philosopher lay fully clothed, with a scarf around his neck, under the covers. He sat up and extended his arms as I approached. I bent down and we embraced one another ardently. Then he held me away at arm's length and studied my face as I studied his.

"But your color is good," he said with some astonishment. "You look better than I expected."

"And you look marvelous," I said. We promptly abandoned the tone that had prompted our meeting — the belief that both of us would be dead before too long and that this was our last time together alive.

We sensed a great and explosive joy to be together and we talked like two gossips — about Pierre Reverdy, about René Schwob — he urged me to translate *Moi Juif* and to contact the Gruneliuses for biographical information for an introduction.

I began to take my cameras out on the side of his bed. He looked at them with loathing. We had agreed beforehand that I would photograph him.

"All right," he said. "But you don't know how I dislike being photographed. Only three pictures — and please shoot fast so we get this over."

"I dislike being photographed, too," I told him. "But afterward we will be glad we did it."

"Glad to preserve this ugly face. . . ."

"In this light, your face is beautiful," I said.

"You don't need flash?"

"No—the light is perfect," I said as I began shooting.

"Wait—I'm not ready," Jacques protested.

"If I wait until you are ready, Jacques, I'll get nothing but dead photographs," I said.

His face softened with astonishment, perplexity, resignation and I got what I felt would be a good photograph.

I engaged him in rapid conversation and continued shooting.

"But you are machine-gunning me," he said finally. "That is surely more than three photos."

"I have to waste a lot of film to get three good ones from someone so camera shy," I explained.

The fragrance of meat and vegetables floated up the stairwell from the kitchen and we prepared to go down for lunch. He turned toward me, holding a lap-blanket in his hands, and said: "Before we go down, I need to talk to you about something. I have a friend here, a composer who was once famous. He lives here in the house and will join us for lunch. Always you ask what you can do for me. The best thing you can do for me is to help my friend. His works are not played. He lives here as a recluse, completely unknown and in despair. Raïssa loved his work. You might know his name—Arthur Lourié."

"You mean Lourié is alive," I said. "And living here?"

"You know of him, then?"

"Of course—but I had no idea. . . . It's been years."

It turned out that the lady who had let me in and who was cooking our lunch was Lourié's wife, Elizabeth. They were old and cherished friends of the Maritains. Jacques had discovered them living in misery in New York and had invited them to move to Princeton and live in his house permanently.

Downstairs, Jacques presented me to Arthur Lourié who appeared astonished that I should even know his name. We went into the dining room for a simple but magnificent lunch of *pâté*, spinach, hot smoked tongue with horseradish, potatoes, cheese and breads and coffee.

We talked music, Jacques urging the conversation toward Lourié. Madame Lourié joined tremulously, as though she were handling a delicate subject that could disintegrate at any moment.

How could we let the world know that Arthur was still alive, still composing, and would like to have contact with colleagues in music? His great champions in the U.S., Koussevitsky and Engels (of Schirmer) were dead. We decided the best thing I could do would be to write an article about him.

"Perhaps you could make some photographs of Arthur while you are here — to illustrate the article," Jacques suggested. And when Lourié recoiled slightly at the suggestion, Jacques, who had been so reluctant before my cameras an hour earlier, assured him. "Of course you must. John is a fine photographer. Why, he's been photographing *me* all morning."

An extraordinary atmosphere existed in those rooms during those hours — an atmosphere of unguarded tenderness for one another, utterly open and without facade. It was as though I were there with three people shut off from the world and I alone had access to the world that would open some doors for Lourié. Madame Lourié trembled with hope and excitement, hovering in the background, offering to fetch me endless glasses of apple juice or anything I could desire.

She kept getting me aside to express her longing that I could do them that "favor." I assured her I would be doing the world a favor to get some of Arthur's music played again. We photographed Arthur and Jacques together for a long time and we discussed what music was available for performance. A violin concerto. I told him I would send it to Isaac Stern and take a copy with me to Europe to give to Lola Bobesco. A new work in progress for cello and orchestra. Certainly, I assured him, Zara Nelsova would be interested in seeing it. And then I began to perceive the difficulties we might face. Arthur, Jacques explained quietly, could be very "difficult" about performances of his work. Once when Koussevitsky had introduced one of his major works in Boston and the audience applauded and called for the composer, Lourié was coaxed on stage to share the honors with Koussevitsky. He chose that moment of triumph to tell Koussevitsky, "It's inconceivable that anyone could play my work so badly."

So, when I suggested contemporary performers who might be interested in seeing his newer works, Lourié confessed that he had lived in seclusion so long he no longer knew the names of current master performers. "Can you assure me that they are not only first class virtuosos but also musicians of profound quality?" he asked. I assured him, somewhat shaken, that people like Isaac Stern, Lola Bobesco and Zara Nelsova were "finished artists" of the highest calibre.

The time was going. I begged them to excuse me, explaining I had to go photograph Ashley-Montagu and that we had better bring this visit to an end.

No, Jacques wondered if I could not come back for supper and then we could hear some recordings of Lourié's work. I said I'd like nothing better and would return providing Jacques would go to bed as he was supposed to right after supper and leave the Louriés and me to listen to the music.

I took the cab to Ashley-Montagu's and there we got into a long conversation about physical phenomena sometimes seemingly connected with the mystical life — a subject of great interest to him from the purely medical and scientific viewpoint. During our conversation I photographed him and he was marvelously cooperative. He presented a problem however. He is physiologically such a beautiful specimen that the beauty tends to mask the character and personality that is clearly there. How to keep such a man from looking so much like a matinée idol that his real self is obscured? I am not at all sure I succeeded.

His house was full of light — a great contrast to the darkness of the Maritain home with its heavy furniture, its ikons, its sense of silence and seclusion.

I returned to Maritain's house for supper with Jacques and the Louriés. We ate soup, fish, cauliflower, with bread and cheese in the kitchen — an extraordinary kitchen completely painted with frescos of French scenes. During the war when Jacques and Raïssa were so homesick for France, their friend, the noted painter André Girard, came and painted their walls with scenes from France.

Shortly after supper, we embraced Jacques and he went upstairs to retire. Arthur and I went into the living room where he set up an excellent portable phonograph and prepared to play some recordings made live at various performances of his works. He got out the scores to the works, seated me on a sofa and we prepared to listen.

First there was a splendid performance of *De Ordinatione Angelorum* for chorus and brass orchestra, performed by Ross and the Schola Cantorum. It was a work of the most sublime beauty and originality. After a brief moment, Jacques reappeared in the doorway, his forefinger to his lips to silence us. He seated himself in an upholstered chair beside the sofa. We understood. He could not bear to miss the music. We propped a chair under his feet and put a lap-robe over him.

I followed the music in score while Jacques lay there almost completely inert, all attention focused on the sounds.

A slight motion at the door leading into the kitchen attracted my glance and I looked up in time to see Madame Lourié, an expression of frightful anguish on her face, draw back out of sight. Occasionally she would peer around the door facing, apparently to see if I liked the music.

I was devastated by the grandeur and originality of this work — so much so that when it was over, I could find no words to express my admiration. I muttered something about its being magnificent, laid the score beside me on the sofa and moved through the door to the kitchen to get a drink of water.

Jacques Maritain with
composer Arthur Lourié
in Maritain's home at
Princeton, New Jersey

The tiny, frail figure of Madame Lourié followed me in the half light, and once in the kitchen she grasped my hands in hers, looked up at me with tear-flooded eyes, and asked: "What do you think? Is it good?"

I bent down and kissed her cheek. "Good? Why it's a very great work, a great and magnificent and overwhelming work," I said.

"Why didn't you tell him so?" she sobbed.

"He composed it. He must know," I protested. "Surely no one needs to tell him."

"He doesn't know. He needs to know. Please tell him. Give him some encouragement."

"Dear Lord—come in with us. I'll tell him," I said. I led her into the living room and told Lourié what I had told her, feeling like a fool to be saying something so obvious. There was something hideously wrong in all this. Here a master musician and composer — so long unplayed, so surrounded by silence while everyday dung music is performed and recorded. A master was playing home-made recordings of masterworks for me, but not, alas, in the sense of giving me a privilege. No, I realized he was *auditioning* — humbly — hoping I might help him to get performances once again. It was so obscene, in a sense, that he should humiliate himself in this manner that I choked on my words.

He put on *Le Festin pendant la peste* for soprano solo, chorus and full orchestra, a suite from his opera — again an extraordinary masterwork. It spoke so directly, so originally, with its metallic textures and sublime cantilena that I abandoned the score and just let the music absorb me. Jacques lay back in his chair, waxen, immobile, in an attitude of such abandonment to the music that for a moment I was frightened, thinking he had expired. But during the *Aria de Mary*, sung by Galina Vishnevskaya, at a point where the melody soars to eloquence, Jacques' bony hand reached over and rested on my arm.

At the end, Jacques roused himself and opened his eyes. He remarked that for all its originality and contemporary tonality parts of the work reminded him of illuminated manuscript, with the brasses like gold leaf.

October 28, 1962   My daughter Susan's first communion. I returned to Jacques and we went by taxi to Mass at the Aquinas Institute with Arthur and Elizabeth. We offered our Masses for Susan's intentions. Returned afterward for breakfast and then they began to question me about racism in America. I told them about Clyde Kennard's situation. Jacques, stricken with anguish, clutched his chest and had to be taken up to bed to rest from the emotion.

I speak of his frailty and physical weakness, but in truth there is a sub-stratum of strength, toughness, and an illusion of wit and tenderness at the same time. A tremendous force lies behind that frailty.

I left them at noon, laden with Arthur's scores and many rolls of exposed film.

Note   I returned to Princeton often after that, even when Jacques was absent, to visit with Arthur and Elizabeth Lourié. Many musicians expressed the deepest interest in Lourié's work after I made it known that he was alive and living in Princeton. Some even went to call on him, to pay him homage, but his reticence could not be overcome. Even though he welcomed the idea of visits from his colleagues in music, at the last moment he would always find an excuse not to receive them. He died in Princeton in 1966 during Jacques Maritain's last visit to the U.S.

Fort Worth

September 30, 1966   JACQUES FLIES from Paris to New York today, and will come here to visit us Monday. We are looking forward to this as one of the high points of our lives. Must get in the foods we will need to prepare. Will make *pâté* tonight.

October 2, 1966   Received telegram last night that Jacques had arrived safely and the plans are all right. So that means he will arrive here tomorrow afternoon, accompanied by Elizabeth Manuel, the daughter of old family friends.

I keep feeling I have left undone some important things, but cannot think what they might be. I have the kinds of foods Jacques can handle, have plenty of films, the cameras are clean, his room will be fixed this evening, the children have been properly threatened with mayhem if they do not behave and remain quiet while he is here, defrosted the refrigerator and will make mayonnaise this afternoon. My only real worry about all this is going to meet him at the Dallas airport. Confined to this wheelchair, I am not really able to go that far without severe pain and fatigue.

October 10, 1966   I begin these notes to cover last week's visit with Jacques because I had no time to make them while we were together.

He and Babeth Manuel flew here on Monday, October 3rd. I was too sick to meet them, so Piedy and Brad Daniel drove over to bring them from the airport. I expected to see him arrive devastated from the trip, and had his room prepared so he could lie down and recover. But not at all. He had no interest in going to bed. He came into his room, leaned back against the desk and began talking. Although attempts had been made to keep his visit to this country a secret, *National Catholic Reporter* had found out and had contacted him about sending a reporter to interview him. He ducked it by telling Robert Hoyt, the editor, that he was on his way to visit me, and that I could write the story, but he would not have time to see anyone else. He explained all of this rapidly to me.

"But I promised you I would never write about you during your lifetime," I said.

"Well, someone will, and I would rather it be you. Besides, I am so near dead it doesn't really make that much difference now," he said, looking more alive than I ever remembered seeing him.

We gave him the boys' room at the back of the house, next to my office. There he had a quiet place of privacy, with a bath—a place to which he could retire whenever he wished. Babeth Manuel shared Susan's room at the front of the house.

We visited, had a supper of tongue, spinach and *crème au caramel* and after supper we went through his new article in *Nova et Vetera*, an important theological study entitled *De la grâce et de l'humanité de Jésus.*

Just before retiring, Jacques asked us to show him where to find the coffee makings and some bread and cheese. We arranged to leave him as free as possible, so he could get up whenever he wished, (early), prepare his own coffee, have his breakfast of bread and cheese. Then, he would join us toward noon. We would take lunch and supper together.

Jacques visited with his latest godchild, our daughter, Amanda, but since she still slept much of the time, his visits were mostly a matter of looking down into her crib, watching her sleep and being careful to hold his pipe away so the ashes would not fall on her bedclothes.

Tuesday was mercifully free of visitors, a quiet, rainy day. It gave us the opportunity to settle into a routine, get some rest, get over the excitement of having Jacques in our home. We talked and rested and I made some photographs of Jacques and the baby, Jacques with Babeth and all of them together talking.

At the noon meal, we talked about Reverdy and his great love for Raïssa's work. Babeth remarked that although she loved Raïssa's poems, she had never been able to "understand" Reverdy's work. I went to fetch a volume of Reverdy's poems and Jacques read them, sitting at the table after the meal. Just to hear him read them was enough to make them perfectly comprehensible to anyone.

After lunch, Jacques asked me to come to his room, where he gravely inquired what he could do for his godchild, Amanda. "Give me some ideas," he said. "I am nil when it comes to choosing some appropriate gift."

Jacques Maritain holding his goddaughter, Amanda Griffin, Texas

30

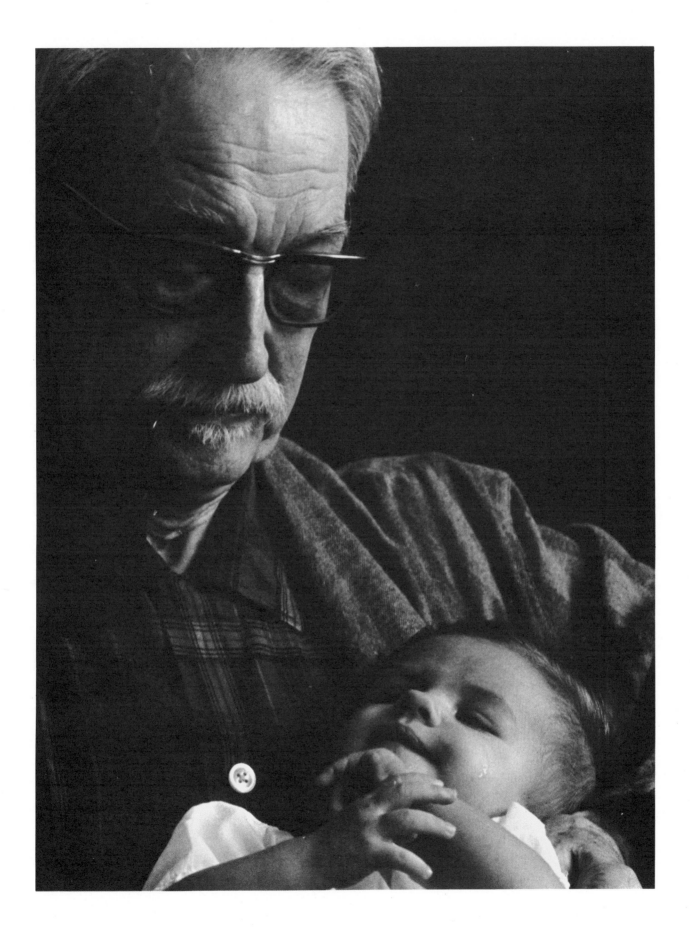

I suggested that perhaps the most cherished gift would be a tape recording of his reading the poems of Reverdy as he had just done at table. He liked the idea and we decided to make an hour's tape—with Jacques reading the poems of Reverdy on one side and those of Raïssa on the other. I was ready to begin, but as with all things, Jacques had to prepare very carefully. He asked me for copies of Raïssa's works and of Reverdy's; and he spent much of the afternoon reading them, marking the ones he would record. Later, we heard him singing through the closed door of his room—he was practising two of Raïssa's canticles to put on the tape also.

Tuesday evening the noted Mexican conductor, Luis Berber, and his wife, Wilenne, came to supper, along with Brad Daniel. Jacques felt in the mood to cook, so we put an apron on him and he prepared a large serving of eggs *à la Mère Poulard* with all of the temperament, fire and nervosity of a Brillat-Savarin.

Knowing we would have many guests on Wednesday, we got up early and began the recordings. Jacques read Raïssa's work on one side of a tape—almost an hour. This was emotionally exhausting for him, so we decided to wait until later to record the Reverdy portion.

Jacques rested until noon, preparing the things he would say to a group of philosophers and theologians, seven Basilian Fathers who were to fly in from St. Thomas University in Houston for a brief visit in the afternoon. Around two in the afternoon, Father George Curtsinger, Dr. Eugene Curtsinger and Dr. Allen Reid arrived for a brief visit. Jacques, mistaking them for the Basilian Fathers from Houston, launched into a little speech about the condition of the Church and contemporary theology and then asked them how things were in Houston. They looked blank. I explained that they were not from Houston, but from this area, and that Dr. Reid had been helping me a great deal with my physical problems. At this, Jacques, embarrassed at his error, grabbed Dr. Reid's hands, brought them to his lips and kissed them ardently, thanking him for helping me with my illness. Dr. Reid turned scarlet to receive such homage from a man he so deeply revered, and the three visitors soon left.

The Basilian Fathers arrived shortly thereafter, all of them either old friends of Jacques, or former students or colleagues. They had promised to stay only a half-hour. It was a splendid reunion and Jacques reveled in such companionship. We really wanted them to remain longer, but they were firm and left exactly when they had promised they would. Another close friend, Father August Thompson, arrived from Louisiana and remained with us. Then later in the evening, Penn Jones came with Edward Keating, the editor and owner of *Ramparts* magazine.

Suddenly, Jacques was pale and without strength. The day had been too strenuous. We got him to bed and the rest of us sat up and talked until late. It had been decided that Penn Jones, our old friend from Midlothian, Texas, editor of the Midlothian newspaper, would "take" Jacques and me to Gethsemani so that Jacques and Thomas Merton could have what would surely be their last visit together. Since I was badly crippled from foot surgery and Jacques was weak, we could not hope to go without someone to help us, and Penn agreed to be that person.

On Thursday morning we completed the recording early. At ten a.m., Penn Jones came to take us to the airport, where we caught a flight to Louisville. There, we met another old friend, Fr. J. Stanley Murphy, C.S.B., who had flown down from Canada to join us. In a rented car, Penn Jones drove us to the Abbey of Gethsemani, at Trappist, Kentucky.

The countryside around the abbey was beautiful. We arrived in the softest autumn dusk. Merton stood by the gatehouse, waiting for us with a wheelchair, dressed in his black and white monastic robes with a faded blue denim jacket and a black woolen peacap.

Penn Jones,
Fr. J. Stanley Murphy,
C.S.B., and Daniel Walsh
with Jacques Maritain,
Thomas Merton's
hermitage, Gethsemani,
Kentucky

They helped me into the wheelchair and took me to my room first. Then Merton showed the rest of the guests to their rooms. Penn returned to help me unpack, and had hardly finished before we were called to join Fr. Abbot James Fox in a small private dining room on the main floor. Thomas Merton,

Fr. Stan Murphy, Penn Jones, Jacques and I arranged ourselves around the dinner table with Abbot Fox. Here the conversation was timid, though I could see Merton's impatience to plunge into something solid with Jacques. Jacques and Tom continually lapsed into French, and then Jacques would apologize to the Abbot, who soon assured him that he understood French well enough, knew it was a strain for Jacques to speak English, and urged us to continue in French without any concern for him.

We were served soup, steak, vegetables, salad and dessert, with wine. I relished this for Merton. Trappists do not take meat, and I wondered how long it had been since he had tasted steak and when, if ever, he would taste it again. He consumed it with enthusiasm.

Father Abbot excused himself to go to bed, since the community rises at three-fifteen a.m. He gave Merton permission to sleep in a little later, so the monk remained with us. We went to Jacques' room for a bull session. There we talked of Jacques' new book and he gave a set of page proofs to Merton. But since we were all tired from the trip, and since Merton is accustomed to retiring around 7:30 p.m., we did not linger very long. At 8:30 we fixed Jacques a glass of bourbon and left him.

Penn and Fr. Stan wheeled me down the corridor to my room, really the bishop's quarters, a small three-room suite with sleeping room, sitting room and bath. Jacques had almost identical quarters at the other end of the hall.

The guestmaster met us in the hall and suggested that he awaken us for the 5:15 conventual Mass. This was to take place in a provisional chapel on the third floor, since the abbey church was being completely remodeled. We agreed. He said I could sit in my wheelchair at the stairwell and hear it; and the others could join the community for the celebration.

Before sleeping, I lay in bed and listened to a silence that seemed to roar, relieved by a distant screech owl in the woods.

They awakened me the next morning at 4:45. I dressed, threw some water on my face and was trying to spread up my bed when two monks came in and told me they had found a way to take me up on a freight elevator so I could assist at Mass after all in the chapel. They helped me down a small flight of steps (carried me in the wheelchair) and wheeled me through the dim-lit kitchens. We went up one story on the freight elevator and then they wheeled me through vast rooms—the monks' refectory, the dormitories and library to another elevator which took me up to the third floor. It was an extraordinary trip, in complete silence and near darkness through those labyrinths within the cloister.

Conventual Mass, chanted in English, was beautiful.

At six they took me back through those long spaces to my room. A monk came, told me Merton would join me for breakfast, and asked what I would like. I told him some eggs and coffee would be fine. He said the other guests would go downstairs to eat in the guesthouse dining room, but that he would bring breakfast for two to my room in a few moments.

Merton appeared with him and they unloaded the breakfast cart and set the table together. They remembered from previous visits that I am diabetic and added special dietetic food to the breakfast tray.

When the other monk had gone, Merton took a seat at the table and we uncovered our dishes—mine had a large rasher of bacon and eggs, his only some eggs. I told him in dismay that I was not allowed any pork, and offered him my bacon, which he accepted almost before I had finished speaking.

Later, when the monk returned to get the dishes, he asked me if the breakfast had been satisfactory and if I wanted anything else.

"No, it was wonderful," I said, and then was inspired to add: "Perhaps just a little more bacon in the morning, if you don't mind."

At 7:30 all of us met at the gatehouse and arranged for cars to take us up to Merton's hermitage in the woods. Merton had a large water jug (since he has no water at the hermitage) and Jacques was warmly dressed with his lap-robe folded over his arm, beaming with the joy of the morning. Drs. Dan Walsh and Jack Ford joined us and we took our cameras up to that isolated spot in the forest where Merton has his cabin. It was a perfect autumn morning, brilliantly clear, cold and fragrant.

The men carried me inside and got me settled in a chair. Merton added fuel to build up a large wood-burning fire in the hearth. He placed Jacques in a rocking chair very near the fire and tucked the lap-robe around his legs. Here the conversation sprang into full vitality immediately. Jacques and Merton had much to discuss. I photographed without much talking and so did Penn Jones.

Merton told us about his work—he was doing a study on Bob Dylan.* He explained to Jacques and me that Dylan was an important new voice, a poet and song-writer. Merton demonstrated for us, putting on one of the Dylan records, HIGHWAY 61. This music blared forth at top volume through the great pine forest. Merton explained that Father Abbot let him have the phonograph and recordings for research on this article, and that soon he would have to return them. He glowed with pleasure at the music, translating rapidly the language that was largely lost to us under the accompaniment. The music and

*This study was requested by *Jubilee* magazine, whose editors provided the recordings, but the project was never completed, though Merton's interest in the work of Dylan remained strong to the end of his life.

especially the words got us into high key, a high key that was truly strange for a man with Jacques' tastes. Jacques was, however, open to it. I found it almost unbearable in that setting. And I was greatly relieved to discover that Merton did not intend to play more after that record was finished.

When it was over, Merton fixed us some coffee in the two cups he possessed and in some plastic glasses. Then he offered to read some of his new experimental poetry. He read mostly from a series he called *Edifying Cables.* In it, images that have no apparent connections clash against one another to make connections and produce an effect of enormous vitality and brilliance. Jacques was very taken with it, and almost simultaneously we remarked that although it was completely unlike the work of Reverdy, still the one brought the other to mind.

At ten thirty we got back into the cars and returned down the hill to the abbey where Merton celebrated Mass (in Latin, for Jacques' sake) in a small temporary chapel out behind a wall near the cemetery, a beautiful inverted

Jacques Maritain, Rev. J. Stanley Murphy, C.S.B., Penn Jones, Thomas Merton and Daniel Walsh on a picnic at Gethsemani, Kentucky

36

V-shaped structure. He asked me to photograph this Mass. It was a slow, leisurely ceremony, full of the old touches, and we were profoundly caught up in it—not because it was in the old style, but because it was so unmistakably thoughtful in being geared to Jacques' age and habits. Jacques remained for a long time afterward in thanksgiving, without moving, without taking his eyes from the altar.

Jacques Maritain with
Thomas Merton in
Merton's hermitage,
Abbey of Gethsemani,
Trappist,
Kentucky, 1966

We returned to the guesthouse to have lunch with Father Abbot in that same small private room: fish, cauliflower, potatoes, soup, a salad, white wine. We discussed the vernacular translations. Jacques, who was by now thoroughly in favor of such translations, nevertheless lamented some of them, and he cited, as an example of abominable rendering, the new French version of the parable of the wise and foolish virgins, in which foolish virgins is given as *les vièrges étourdies* (scatter-brained, dizzy, confused).

After lunch, Jacques began to wander toward my room (his was at the other end of the hall). We got him straightened out and headed in the right direction. He mumbled apologetically to Merton, *"Je suis un peu étourdi aujourd'hui..."* (I'm a little confused today).

To which Merton, spontaneously and sympathetically, replied, "Yes, Jacques . . . like the virgins."

After a brief rest, we met at 1:30 in the afternoon and went in cars to the woods near a lake. There, they spread blankets on the ground and sat among the trees. Penn Jones and Jack Ford went to get some beer and paper cups. I loaded the Alpa 6C for Merton who loved to make photographs with this great instrument.

Merton and I photographed for a while as he carried on a running conversation with Jacques. When the drinks were ready and served, along with sacks of peanuts, their conversation began in earnest — talk about the Vietnam war and also about the loss of individual privacy in the computer age. Merton suggested that the time was not far away when even our travel will be reported — every time a man buys an airline ticket, the information will be fed to computers in Washington so that men will be known wherever they go and in all their activities.

Much of the conversation was confidential, frank discussions of bishops, theologians and other churchmen.

Late in the afternoon we packed the ice buckets and cameras and returned to the Abbey, exhausted and elated with the perfection of the day. We took supper with Father Abbot again — salmon loaf, salad, vegetables, white wine — at five p.m. Then they took me to my room. The others accompanied Jacques to the Chapter Room where he addressed the whole monastic community.

At seven they returned. I went down the hall to tell Jacques good night. He was chagrined, thinking he had not talked well, but with reassurances from Merton, Penn Jones, Father Stan, he was soon placated. He said he was going to smoke a pipe and then retire.

The others returned with me to my room, promising ourselves to break it up not later than 8 p.m. It occurred to us that Jacques would certainly welcome a glass of whiskey after the strain of his address to the community. Penn Jones fixed a glass of bourbon and water, carried it to him and returned astonished at the ardor of Jacques' gratitude for the inspired charity.

We were awakened at 5:30 Saturday morning, hurried to dress and go to the small private chapel where Merton again celebrated Mass for us. It was quite dark and very cold.

We concluded Mass as the sun rose on a crisp morning of great clarity. The others went downstairs to breakfast. Merton had breakfast in my room with me, hardly able to consume the double rasher of bacon the kitchen sent up. We discussed our future plans, our work. Later, after packing, we met in one of the parlors at the gatehouse where Merton and Maritain talked of "chemical mysticism" and "the religion of LSD."

When it was time to leave, Father Abbot Fox came to tell us good-bye. He had arranged for a Brother to guide us to the new highway, which would simplify our trip into the Louisville airport.

Madame Grunelius with village children, Château de Kolbsheim, France

Kolbsheim

July 28, 1967   Left DALLAS YESTERDAY and arrived in Paris at 6:30 a.m. A wheel-chair was waiting. Spent the day with Babeth Manuel and Jacques Deschanel of Desclée de Brouwer. They returned me to Orly for the 9:15 p.m. flight to Strasbourg where Alexandre Grunelius met me and brought me here. We arrived before eleven and I was greeted warmly by Antoinette Grunelius who told me Jacques was waiting up to see me. She took me back to his room for a brief visit. We embraced, and as soon as Jacques had made certain I had survived the trip, he insisted that I have some food.

When I told him I was not going to ask for food at that hour of the night, he got up and accompanied me back through the corridors to the salon where he asked Antoinette if she could not offer me something to eat. She had already laid out a small supper, a splendid *oeuf gelé*, with bread, butter, cheese and wine.

After a brief conversation, Antoinette and Alexandre showed me to my rooms. I have now unpacked and am ready for bed. They have given me a splendid downstairs apartment. Everything is touching, especially after twenty-four hours with no sleep. A bowl of roses here on my writing table, the bed made back, some toasts and diabetic preserves. In the profound silences of the country at midnight, nerves relax into peace. Great joy in being here again, in seeing Jacques so lively and superb.

July 29, 1967

Slept deeply until eight a.m. Got up, opened the shutters to a magnificent view of the gardens, formal, trimmed hedges and great blotches of flowers and softened by a light mist. Made coffee with tap water from the bathroom. I sit here in the silences of the country, relishing the light, the peace, the rest.

Later

Now, absolute stillness. The sun's brilliance filters through the clouds. Soaked flowers in the garden release fragrance, and a dense droning of bees underlines the chirping of birds.

They have brought my breakfast, silently, leaving it beside the door in the corridor. It is a beautiful sight — a brown earthenware pitcher filled with coffee, a white pitcher filled with scalded milk, some melba toast and some brown bread, a saucer of sweet butter and a pot of raspberry preserves (diabetic — the first I have ever tasted that I really like). I am overwhelmed that the Gruneliuses would even remember I am diabetic. But unobtrusive thoughtfulness is the tone of this great household — it has been raised to a high art. Everything is provided. It is simply there. And this includes the supreme luxury of solitude. They leave you alone. You get together for meals and a short visit in the evening, otherwise, you are free.

Strange how the view of everything is heightened in this subdued atmosphere. The most ordinary objects take on a special visual beauty. One has a sense of time (even on an otherwise rushed schedule of work), time to look and see.

Jacques Maritain at table
with Madame Grunelius,
Kolbsheim

Now, later, I have not been able to resist and have photographed from my open windows the gardens and the countryside beyond. The bell from the chapel tower clangs twice for the half-hour at 10:30 a.m.

Evening: Jacques and I worked well this afternoon, and I have worked on alone until now, 7 p.m. A profound stillness of twilight over the countryside. Flowers enter still radiant into the obscurity.

Bells from the chapel announce 8:30 p.m. A child was wounded this evening, not seriously, but Antoinette has taken him in to the hospital. Supper is delayed. We wait in a great silent château. Jacques brought me some bourbon. I am hungry. We pray everything is all right for the child. Alexandre, whom we call Lexi, has gone to get me a wheelchair. This château is so large I need one to go the distance to the salons and dining area.

I walked, taking my time, to the salon, practiced Couperin on the Pleyel and read some in *Figaro Littéraire.*

How to describe Jacques' physical regime? He eats very little, takes coffee, bourbon with sugar, smokes a pipe — a combination that stimulates his mind and fatigues his frail body. I try it this evening and am in a sort of euphoria, working well, but aware also of a great animal need to eat and then to sleep.

Jacques Maritain in discussion with Alexandre Grunelius, Kolbsheim, France

At 6:30 a.m., the blinds are opened to hazed sunlight — a view over the gardens and across the valley — greenery, flowers, slanted first rays of the sun. All the bells in the valley sound continuously from churches in nearby villages.

July 30, 1967

These sights and sounds enter profoundly into my being, make me part of them and restore me to nature — in the manner of a deep nostalgia that somehow materializes into the experience about which one was nostalgic. If only my family were here. That is the only blemish.

Lexi rented a splendid wheelchair with rubber bicycle tires yesterday, so I can move silently and freely now.

Breakfast has come. I wait to go to 8:15 Mass in the chapel next door. The bells begin even as I write this.

Jacques Maritain and Alexandre Grunelius, Kolbsheim

A village Mass that was for me new in tone—a Mass really for the children. The priest talked simply, warmly and lovingly—and without formality, as though we were members of his family. It was a bilingual Mass, in French and German, German for the elderly and also to keep the sound in the ears of the children. I attended in the wheelchair. Lexi rolled me back here afterward and the priest followed to greet me and talk for a moment.

Later—5 p.m.

Worked all day retranslating the Bible quotes. Jacques translated directly from the Vulgate. As we worked, Jacques grumbled, "They should pay us a translation fee."

Jacques has insisted on arranging for a famed homeopathic specialist who has done him much good, to examine me. He is due to arrive shortly. He is so famous that tomorrow evening German TV is to do a feature documentary on his work.

Have not had time to write the letters I intended to write today. Now, I wait for the doctor. It is warm, calm; the view especially beautiful from my window.

Night

Monsieur Mésségué, the healer, with two of his colleagues and Jacques gathered here in the room where the three healers examined me closely. Monsieur Mésségué, a man of great elegance and charm, said he could do nothing for the diabetes, but would treat me for the circulation problems and tumors. Jacques is delighted, and considers this meeting providential. At supper, we discussed the examination. Monsieur Mésségué's clients include many of the great names of France: Jean Cocteau, the Mauriac family, etc. He is noted for charging enormous fees even for examination. This frightened me, but apparently he has assured them he does not intend to charge me anything.

July 31, 1967

Up at six, but slow to wake—black coffee and medicine and sat in front of the window and read the Mass for today as church bells rang, watched the countryside stir to life, heard the doves.

More coffee. Have shaved and now at 7:30 am ready to begin work.

Jacques is finding many errors in the work, errors that I missed.

Good work finally. Good letters from home.

Monsieur Méssegué came again. He and Jacques talked in my room while Méssegué, seeming to pay little attention to me, examined me quite thoroughly from head to foot, mostly looking and placing his hands on me to get the "vibrations"(?). The whole time he was manipulating me, flipping me over like a dead whale, he chatted with Jacques. I felt like telling him to pay some attention to what he was doing.

Later — 11:35

He is a charmer, though, a man with an irresistible flair. He has been tried in France for his practices, but the judge who condemned him and found him guilty, at the same time announced he was becoming Méssegué's patient; and the prosecuting attorney wrote the preface to one of his books; and the president of the Academy of Medicine wrote the preface to another. When he left, he said that he would treat me for six or eight months, sending along the herbal medications I would need as I needed them; and he promised I could lead a more or less normal life if I followed his instructions carefully. He reminded us to be sure and watch the TV special this evening.

We gathered after supper, Lexi, Antoinette and I, in the TV room to watch the documentary on Monsieur Méssegué, which turned out to be the cruelest possible documentary against him, with towering denunciations from German doctors and health authorities; analyses showing his products were 85 percent water. We were glad Jacques had not remained up to see it. This is really an embarrassing situation. Certainly Méssegué had been led to believe the documentary was favorable, since he had urged us to watch. It turned out to be a total condemnation of the man and his work, and a viciously slanted one, too. It emphasized scenes from his life of wealth and leisure, in a fabulous home on the Mediterranean, surrounded by beautiful women and famous guests, a deliberate distortion really, since the scenes were not his home and the producers made it appear they were. A real character assassination.

Night

Up at 6:30 and to work immediately. Much, much work, but I sleep well and am well, so it is a joy. Jacques is disconsolate because we have to work so hard and urges me to take time off to go into the gardens, but he will not take off a single moment for himself and is pale and weak.

August 1, 1967

August 3, 1967 Early breakfast finished, but with a large cup of coffee and milk here at my elbow. Work constantly. We are one/fourth done now. IBM sent a typewriter from Paris with an American keyboard. It goes better.

Some guests have come: the Grunelius's marvelous daughter, Odile and her husband Dr. Claude Sebenne, a distinguished physicist. They light up the place

Msgr. Jacques de Menasce in conversation with Jacques Maritain, Kolbsheim

with their youthful beauty, their kindness and charm. Odile keeps me supplied with fresh coffee and fresh flowers.

During the rain yesterday I made many photos.

August 7, 1967 Have neglected the journal since the typewriter arrived because we have been working constantly and without a moment's pause except for meals. Jacques is rewriting a great deal in English, and this makes for pages that only he or I could decipher, so I am typing them up as rapidly as I can, and some of them are difficult, especially where there are footnotes to be checked for accuracy.

But the weather and the beauty of this place remain splendid. We resent it that we have to work so constantly and so rapidly, because this means that we look at one another and at the magnificent views only obliquely, having no time to sit and relax and talk.

When I am not at this typewriter, I am photographing. Magnificent things to photograph — the light during this season is superbly beautiful.

Today is Antoinette's birthday. I made some birthday pictures, after lunch, of Antoinette, and indeed the whole family, and Jacques too.

This evening, Lexi came to my door and knocked quietly. When I asked him to enter, we immediately began to discuss some of the translation. His English is flawless; I only now realize this, because we have always spoken French. When we had finished, he hesitated a moment, and then remarked that he might have made a little mistake this afternoon.

"The American poet, W. H. Auden was here for a while today. When he heard that you were here, he was most anxious to meet you. I told him we never disturb you at work, and he immediately insisted that I not call you."

The disappointment I felt must have shown on my face, for Lexi said: "I see it was a mistake..."

"A little one," I laughed.

At supper tonight, I learned that Nicholas Nabokov comes tomorrow to spend the week.

Too busy to write in this journal. So only quick notes.   *August 11, 1967*

Nabokov arrived and has been a great help to me, since he speaks all languages (at least all that we need, and is very strong in Latin). He gave me the manuscript of his new symphony, to be premiered by the N.Y. Philharmonic, but the writing is so small I have difficulty with it. We have played a number of his recordings — strong and beautiful music.

Also, poor Antoinette has been kept really busy with Jacques and me and her other guests. We have started my "treatments," foot baths with a lot of herbs in boiling water. She takes care of bringing them to me, and then runs to do whatever the doctor ordered for Jacques. Odile and Claude Sebenne have taken me for several rides in their car to nearby villages to photograph — at Jacques' insistence. We have a couple of English ladies who help with the typing now.

Monsignor Jacques de Menasce is here to liven things up, too. He arrived from Mexico. He is an old and dear friend of Jacques, attached to the Vatican.

Since Jacques is under terrible pressure now, the arrival of Monsignor de Menasce was discussed. He has a way of "stimulating" Jacques into discussion that often turns heated. It was decided that Jacques was in no condition for this kind of ragging, and so when Odile went to get Monsignor at the airport, she explained that he must be "good" and not get Jacques into any arguments.

Monsignor breezed in, kissed Antoinette's hand and said in a loud voice, "Odile tells me I must be good. Madame, I will not be bludgeoned into virtue."

He unloaded his Mexican masks on the sofa, gave me greetings from Anne Freemantle whom he had been visiting in Mexico, and then fell dramatically silent, staring at the salon door. I turned to see it open slowly and Jacques appear in the doorway. In the dim light, Jacques distinguished only the group of us. He began talking with me, looking me in the eyes, while Monsignor prostrated his pudgy figure flat on his belly on the floor at Jacques' feet in a surprisingly agile dive. Jacques did not see him, though Monsignor's forehead was almost touching Jacques' shoes. The others began to titter and Jacques followed our glance down to the black-clad figure at his feet. A smile lighted his face, followed immediately by a fierce expression of feigned episcopal disapproval and he told Monsignor to get up off the floor. The two men embraced with great affection and were almost immediately in heated argument, which meant that Odile's warning had gone unheeded.

That evening, after supper, Monsignor innocently and deliberately made an obtuse theological remark that brought Jacques up in anger. They argued and Monsignor provoked Jacques to deeper repudiation.

Early the next morning, Jacques came to my room, sick with chagrin that he had spoken so sharply to his old and dear friend. I assured him that no one, least of all Monsignor, was offended. We went together to Mass in the private chapel of the château which was to be celebrated by Monsignor. Jacques tried to apologize before Mass but Monsignor did not make himself available. During his homily after the Gospel, addressed to the Gruneliuses, Jacques and me, he very wittily rebutted Jacques and got the last word of the argument because during Mass Jacques could not possibly answer him back.

We have made a great discovery in some of Véra's old trunks — a large cache of drawings and water colors by Gwen John (the sister of Augustus John). When Jacques, Raïssa and Véra were living at Meudon, Gwen John came there to live as a recluse and paint. Véra was kind to her and in gratitude each Monday Gwen John brought or sent a drawing or water color as a gift. Véra saved them, of course, and now they have been found in what is certainly one of the most exciting discoveries in the art world this year. Jacques asked me to photograph them and possibly reproduce them in a book. So, I have spent hours the last two days in my rooms, making careful photographs with the Alpa. This close association with these profoundly moving drawings and paintings has been one of the supreme experiences of my life.

Gwen John 1876-1939 — — — — — — — Augustus John 1878-1961

August 13, 1967

My time is almost up here. I leave tomorrow. The book is nearly done. To make sure I had plenty of coverage of the Gwen John collection, I rephotographed 50 of them today. I hope these photographs will bring some income to the *Jacques and Raïssa Maritain Study Center* which has been established here.

(In January and February 1970, accompanied by my daughter, Susan, I made a research trip to Europe to get photographs and materials for the biography of Thomas Merton. After visits and lectures in Holland and Belgium, we flew to Strasbourg to see the Gruneliuses and then on to Toulouse from where I intended to make the trips into the south of France by rented car. Since Jacques Maritain lives with the Little Brothers at Toulouse, we were invited by Sister Marie-Pascale, superior of a small Dominican house near Jacques' quarters, to stay in the convent and work out from there.)

Toulouse

February 5, 1970

A RRIVED HERE YESTERDAY, after all sorts of delays. We rented a car at the airport and made a wild drive through downtown Toulouse at the busiest hour of the day. We were greeted at the gate of this Dominican convent by one of the Sisters who showed us to our rooms on the ground floor, right next to the convent chapel. This is a true house of silence and prayer, but full of warmth. Sister Marie-Pascale arrived soon and welcomed us. She does most of Jacques' typing, and I have known her a long time by correspondence, so we met almost as brother and sister. She introduced us to the other five Sisters in the small community, and then telephoned to inform Jacques of our safe arrival. I spoke with him on the telephone and we agreed to meet at the Little Brothers for Mass at noon tomorrow, and then a group of Little Brothers wanted Susan and me to stay for lunch in their cabin.

We were very tired, so we retired around ten and slept until almost ten this morning. Visited Jacques in his hermitage at eleven-thirty. A great joy to be together again. He is working on a new book and in his usual torment to get it completed before his strength gives out. We relaxed and gossiped a moment, exchanging news about the Gruneliuses and my family. Then Jacques, Susan and I went to Mass together in a very simple and plain chapel only a few steps away from Jacques' hermitage.

After Mass, we met outside the chapel and made some photographs. Jacques was dressed in a strange, flat cap and a handsome overcoat. Then we walked with him back to his hermitage room, embraced him again, and I photographed the sign on the door of the hermitage:

ICI UN VIEIL ERMITE
ARRIVÉ A LA FIN DE SA VIE

Si sa tête ne vaut plus rien, autant le laisser à ses rêves.

Si vous croyez qu'il a encore quelque chose à faire
alors ayez la charité de consentir à la règle imposée par son travail :

PAS PLUS D'UNE DEMI-HEURE

DE CONVERSATION

Here (lives) an aged hermit
arrived at the end of his life.

If his head is no longer worth anything,
as well leave him to his dreams.

If you believe he still has something to do
then have the charity to observe the rule imposed by his work:

NOT MORE THAN A HALF-HOUR
OF CONVERSATION

After lunch with the Little Brothers, Brother Guy offered to drive us around town in the afternoon with Sister Marie-Pascale.

The Dominican Sisters, under the direction of Sister Marie Vincent, have begun to restore the recently discovered rooms in Toulouse where St. Dominic lived and founded the Dominican Order, where he received his first five companions.

We went there to see it, a profound experience, and I photographed it extensively in black and white and color for the Sisters. While I was working, Brother Guy took Susan in the car to do some shopping.

We returned here at 5:30 this evening. Jacques is coming to have supper with us at 7:30. Tomorrow morning, at Jacques' request, I am to give an address to the Little Brothers, then we will go to Mass and have lunch with them again.

Now, the Sisters are saying Vespers in the chapel beside us. I am so tired from all that walking I can hardly make these notes.

Later

One of the Brothers brought Jacques for supper. He comes here every second night to have a full meal, brings along a small metal container in which he carries some soup back to his hermitage for the following night's supper.

The table in the small dining room was set for Jacques, Susan and me, but we insisted that Sister Marie-Pascale (who was serving us) join us and she consented. We had a superb meal prepared by Sister Emmanuel, who is a fine

cook. I asked Sister Marie-Pascale if the Sisters were having this same menu and she said they were not, but they wanted Jacques to have a hearty meal.

Jacques had a whole list of questions he wanted to ask. He is deeply concerned about the effect of computers in teaching and particularly in philosophy. Will computers make the mind obsolete, he wonders. I sidetracked this to a deeper concern. Will computerized information about people destroy privacy?

Sister Marie-Pascale,
John Howard Griffin and
Jacques Maritain at
dinner, the Dominican
Convent, Toulouse, 1970

No time until today to write anything. This afternoon is dark, rainy. Susan has been writing letters and I have been straightening out my films and camera equipment and my Merton notes. Some Dominican Fathers are coming for tea with us.

February 8, 1970

I gave the conference for the Little Brothers. We have seen Jacques frequently, but for brief visits only.

A lot of requests for lectures have begun coming in, but I am having to refuse them, except for the Dominican college. The food is still remarkable.

Susan Griffin,
Jacques Maritain and
John Howard Griffin,
Toulouse, 1970

When I learned that the Sisters were not eating the same dishes we were, I consulted with one of the Little Brothers and we bought a large leg of lamb, so we ate that with the community today. The community is so small, it makes sense. Jacques urged it, and Sister Pascale was gracious about it. Jacques also put in a word for me, asking Sister Emmanuel to let me work in the kitchen each day with her and learn to make some of the dishes, especially pastry. She cooked the *gigot* superbly — better than any I have ever tasted.

Later

We went into the kitchen after the visit with the Dominican Fathers, to have our first lesson in pastry-making. Sister Marie-Pascale joined us. Sister Emmanuel, vastly amused to be my "professor," tied an apron around my middle and began to instruct me in the art. Susan photographed this first lesson so I would not forget how it was done. After we had worked quite a long time with the pastry, mixing and then chilling it, we decided to make a French version of pizza, filling the shell with sautée'd onions and small sausages and baking it. A great success. We also made mayonnaise to serve with the cold *gigot* for supper.

Now, after that great supper, which Jacques relished (and for which I got all the credit, though Sister Emmanuel guided my hands in every move) the Sisters are chanting the night office. Susie and I have closed the blinds in our rooms against the night. Strange and wonderful to be in such a convent. Forgot to mention that the Sisters earn most of their living by weaving the most beautiful cloths, vestments, napkins, etc. They have been getting Susan to help them on the looms, and she is learning.

Jacques Maritain with Frère Heintz at the Little Brothers compound, Toulouse

Photographed Susan and the Sisters in the weaving room this morning. Splendid light from a window in the ceiling. In the afternoon, we visited with Jacques and then with Brother Heintz who is a young, unassuming man of great openness. He is the superior here and Jacques says he has the most gifted philosophic mind he has ever encountered, a sort of genius. You would never guess it because he is so direct and simple in his manner. He drove us to visit some of the Little Brothers' hermitages in the hills, truly poor and simple affairs. We stopped on our way back to visit the Little Sisters and returned just in time for Vespers at the Dominican college.

February 9

Supper here with Jacques. A great evening of talk, mostly about Merton and the work on the biography. Now ready for bed. We go to Prades tomorrow to photograph Merton's birthplace.

Ash Wednesday   Yesterday Susan and I got off to Prades around 9:30. Jacques was tempted to come with us, but we finally decided the drive would be too hard for him. But the drive through the Pyrénées was so beautiful that I was delighted all the way.

It was frustrating only in that I wanted to stop and photograph everywhere and just did not dare take the time.

We had marvelous luck finding the house in Prades. It is virtually unchanged from the views I have seen of it, taken when Merton was an infant there, fifty-four years ago.

Today we went to photograph Montaubin and St. Antonin. That concludes the photographic work on the scenes of Merton's youth, and I am happy. I could not have managed without Susan, who helped with the cameras, the maps, and keeping the expense accounts.

February 12, 1970

A superb supper here with Jacques: oysters, chicken cooked in white wine over onions, good wines. Jacques brought a copy of Raïssa's book on Chagall which he had autographed with great care—a treasure. Susan and I presented Sister Emmanuel with an electric mixer. She was astonished and thrilled.

Jacques Maritain's
hermitage, Toulouse

Jacques and I both feel this may be our last meal together. But we have felt that many times in the past. He is 87. But who knows? He seems indestructible despite his fragility. We may see one another again.

A wholly extraordinary evening. The Sisters chant compline now and Susan and I have just told Jacques good-bye and we prepare our bags. As he left, Jacques asked me to send him some detective books of Rex Stout if I could find any. He remarked with a beaming face that French detective novels were now "unbelievably dirty."

Brother Heintz came to pick Jacques up and tell us good-bye. We embraced as though we would see one another again tomorrow.

I remember the other day, the Dominican Fathers questioned me about Jacques (who lives only a hundred yards from the college) and remarked that I was a *privilégié* since none of them ever get to see him any more. I am aware that I am indeed a *privilégié*, not only to see him, but to see him in these marvelous surroundings.

Jacques Maritain, in his 89th year, was accepted as a novice in the order of The Little Brothers of Jesus at Toulouse. He has recently pronounced his solemn vows as a Little Brother.

EPILOGUE 1973

Jacques Maritain began to fail seriously in March. The edema was visible on his face and hands. Sister Marie-Pascale wrote that he was having to remain in bed more of each day, but remarked that he had suffered such low periods the preceding spring, and had managed to recover.

His last visit to the Dominican Sisters for supper and to work with Sister Marie-Pascale occurred on the evening before Palm Sunday, April 14. He arrived so weak that he almost had to be carried. When the Sisters expressed concern that he should be in bed, he replied with "unbelievable vigor" that he was determined to die on his feet.

He was too weak to leave his hermitage after that, and on Thursday of Holy Week he received the anointing of the sick.

With the accumulation of his mail and other work, he asked Sister Marie-Pascale to come to his hermitage for a work session on Friday, April 27. His last act as an author that evening was to sign a book for a man just released from prison who had discovered his and Raïssa's works while in detention.

When they had finished their tasks, Sister Marie-Pascale tried to leave so Jacques could rest. He urged her to remain for a while. Despite his great physical weakness, he was perfectly lucid and full of youthful enthusiasm for everything they discussed. Much of it was confidential. He talked of his past life, his sense of privilege in having lived so many years with "two saints, Raïssa and Véra." About his condition, he said that the doctor was optimistic. However, Jacques was sure that this was the end and he told Sister Marie-Pascale that he sought only to abandon himself totally to God.

Sister described Jacques, seated in his comfortable chair, all traces of the edema gone from his face and hands, as the embodiment of tenderness and affection. "He was very beautiful," she wrote, "his skin so transparent it appeared to glow from within."

After two hours she told him good-bye and left. The illusion of luminosity led her to understand that they would not see one another again. Jacques appeared to share her intuition.

The next morning, Saturday, he awakened and was helped into his clothes, as usual, by one of the Little Brothers. Almost immediately he fainted. The doctor was summoned and arrived quickly, but his efforts to revive the aged philosopher failed. Jacques died around 7 a.m., April 28, 1973, approximately five months after his 90th birthday.

The following Thursday, May 3, his body, in a simple wooden casket, arrived in Kolbsheim to be buried beside Raïssa. He was accompanied by his religious community, *Les Petits Frères de Jésus*, who carried him immediately into the chapel built by Victor Hammer at the château and placed the coffin on the floor, facing the altar. They expected only a small group at the home of Antoinette and Alexandre Grunelius, the Maritains' devoted friends. But so many came for the funeral that the chapel could not accommodate them. They had to borrow the local Lutheran church for the ceremonies.

Pope Paul sent Monsignor Macchi as his personal delegate, with a chalice for the Grunelius' chapel where Jacques so often prayed. It was used for the first time at the funeral Mass. During these ceremonies, Olivier Lacombe read Jacques' unpublished translation of *The Song of Songs*, and Cardinal Journet read from Jacques' writings on corporal death.

Afterward, the Little Brothers placed the coffin on a small cart and walked with it several miles to the cemetery. The cortege of Jacques' religious brothers and friends moved in silence through the Alsatian countryside on the most ravishing spring afternoon anyone from the area could remember.

At the gravesite, in the quiet of that country cemetery, the "Our Father" was recited in common, followed by a chanted *Salve Regina*.

The small curved concrete bench under a tree at the foot of Raïssa's grave, where Jacques had so often sat, had been lifted to one side when they dug his grave. After the burial, it was carefully replaced to await the visits of Jacques and Raïssa Maritain's friends.

(JHG — June 1973)